Language Arts *for*
Intermediate Students
by Katherine Weitz

BARDS & POETS II
Teaching Helps

Acknowledgements

The art on the cover is "The Death of King Arthur," by 19th century British painter James Archer, courtesy of Wikimedia Commons (commons.wikimedia. org). Other images courtesy of The Graphics Fairy (thegraphicsfairy.com) and Dreamstime (dreamstime.com). Most selections at the beginning of lessons are in the public domain, besides the full length excerpts of the progymnasmata translations, which are used by permission of the Society for Biblical Literature in Atlanta, Georgia (see Bibliography).

I owe a debt of gratitude to several folks for their help on the Cottage Press Language Arts Curriculum. The gorgeous cover designs are the craftsmanship of my friend Jayme Metzgar. Many other dear friends have helped with both editing and content: in particular, Cheryl Turner, Kimberlynn Curles, Dovey Elliott, Kathy Whitmore, Summer Wilkes, Hannah Taylor, Melissa Turner, and all the other exceptional steachers, moms, and students of Providence Prep. My daughter Grace Weitz has spent many hours editing the project, and contributed significantly to the content of Teaching Helps. As always, the main source of help and encouragement in myriad ways – from design consultation to field testing to laundry, dinner, and dish duty – has always come from my dear husband and my wonderful children.—kpw

© Copyright 2020 KP Weitz

Cottage Press

cottagepresspublishing.net

BARDS & POETS II

Teaching Helps Contents

ANSWER KEY

to Selected Exercises

Lesson 1

❧

THE READING MOTHER

I had a mother who read to me
Sagas of pirates who scoured the sea,
Cutlasses clenched in their yellow teeth,
"Blackbirds" stowed in the hold beneath.

I had a Mother who read me lays
Of ancient and gallant and golden days;
Stories of Marmion and Ivanhoe,
Which every boy has a right to know.

I had a Mother who read me tales
Of Gelert the hound of the hills of Wales,
True to his trust till his tragic death,
Faithfulness blent with his final breath.

I had a Mother who read me the things

That wholesome life to the boy heart brings —
Stories that stir with an upward touch,
Oh, that each mother of boys were such!

You may have tangible wealth untold;
Caskets of jewels and coffers of gold.
Richer than I you can never be –
I had a Mother who read to me.

— STRICKLAND GILLILAN

❧

Lesson 1.1

Prose & Poetry

LITERARY ELEMENTS

3 Observe the Invention and Arrangement
◆ **Lyrical Elements**

- He is describing his mother and the stories she read to him.
- He makes you see and hear — both the mother and the stories.
- He compares his mother's legacy of reading to him with a great treasure of jewels and gold.

4 Investigate the Context
◆ **Literary Genre**

- **Genre by literary period** – early 20th century American
- **Genre by poetic/narrative category** – lyrical

Language Logic

HARVEY'S EXERCISE 19

Only review as much as your student needs. You may wish to do just a few from each section over several days. This makes a good classroom exercise as well.

Exercise 19.5

1. I (PRO) do not know where you (PRO) live.

2. Who (PRO) gave her (PRO) that pencil (N)?

3. She (PRO) came from home (N) an hour (N) ago.

4. What (PRO) have you (PRO) there, my (PRO) son (N)?

5. Their (PRO) house (N) is much larger than our (PRO) uncle's. (N)

6. Your (PRO) father (N) is her (PRO) mother's (N) brother.

7. Whose (PRO) farm (N) is for sale in your (PRO) neighborhood? (N)

Exercise 19.6

1. The farmer (N) plows (V) in the spring (N) and fall (N).

2. Their (PRO) father (N) gave (V) them (PRO) money (N).

3. The great tears (N) sprang (V) to their (PRO) eyes (N).

4. They (PRO) followed (V) the cattle (N) home (N).

5. The landlord (N) answered (V) his (PRO) question (N).

6. He (PRO) ordered (V) him (PRO) to go.

7. The pupils (N) who (PRO) had (V) passed (V) a good examination (N), went (V) home (N) with joyful hearts. (N)

Exercise 19.8

1. He who gives (V) cheerfully (ADV) gives twice. (ADV)

2. His affairs were (V) managed (V) imprudently (ADV).

3. Proceed (V) slowly (ADV) and cautiously. (ADV)

4. We shall (V) never (ADV) see (V) his like again. (ADV)

5. You have (V) not (ADV) acted (V) wisely. (ADV)

6. We must (V) study (V) diligently. (ADV)

7. Our dinner, cooked* hastily, (ADV) was (V) eaten (V) greedily. (ADV)

*Cooked is a verbal (participle) here. If a student identifies this as a verb or an adjective, simply explain that it cooked is a verb used as an adjective here, and we will learn more about this later.

Exercise 19.9

1. The boy fell over (PREP) a chair into (PREP) a tub of (PREP) water.

2. I came from (PREP) Boston to (PREP) Cincinnati in (PREP) 1875.

3. We rested by (PREP) the road-side.

4. He walked up (PREP) the valley towards (PREP) the house of (PREP) his friend.

5. Walk with (PREP) me in (PREP) the garden.

6. I went to (PREP) the doctor for (PREP) r advice, but he was not at (PREP) home.

Exercise 19.10

1. He is wise and (CONJ) prudent.

2. James or (CONJ) John will call upon (PREP) you.

3. I study because (CONJ) I wish to learn.

4. Neither Jane nor (CONJ) Sarah was in (PREP) the room.

5. I shall not go, if (CONJ) it rain.

6. He is rich, but (CONJ) is very unhappy.

7. Worship the Lord, for (CONJ) he is our God.

Exercise 19.11

1. Hurrah! (INT) we have won!

2. Pshaw, (INT) that is nonsense.

3. Ha, ha, ha! (INT) I am glad of it.

4. Ahem! (INT) did he say so?

5. "O," (INT) said John.

6. What! (INT) tired so soon ?

HARVEY'S EXERCISE 12

Corrected punctuation shown below.

1. It is a pleasant thing to see the sun. Man is mortal. Flowers bloom in summer.
2. Resolved, that the framers of the Constitution, etc. 3. The town has expended, the past year:

        For grading streets, $15,000.
        For public buildings, 15,000.

4. He said "You are too impulsive."
   Remember the maxim, "A penny saved is a penny earned."
5. "The day is past and gone;
   The evening shades appear;
   0 may we all remember well the night of death draws near."
6. James and Samuel went to Baltimore last August. The general assembly meets on the first Monday in February. 7. The bill was vetoed by the President. John Jones, Esq. Richard the Third. "The opposition was led by Lord Brougham."
8. "When Music, heavenly maid, was young,
   While yet, in early Greece, she sung;
   The Passions, oft, to hear her shell,
   Throng'd around her magic eel . . ."
9. The Central Park ; the Ohio River; I have read "Great Expectations"; The Mountains of the Moon are in Africa. 10. The Lord shall endure forever; Remember thy Creator; Divine love and wisdom; " The ways of Providence."
11. "I know that my Redeemer liveth"; "I am the Way, the Truth, and the Life "; " The Word was made flesh."
12. Those are Chinamen; The Turcomans are a wandering race; The Gypsies of Spain; The Indians are fast disappearing.
13. The Swiss Family Robinson; a Russian serf; "The rank is but the guinea's stamp"; a Cashmere shawl; a Damask rose.
14. The Emancipation Proclamation ; The Art of Cookery; the Missouri Compromise; the Whisky Insurrection ; "A Treatise on the Science of Education and the Art of Teaching."
15. I don't like to study grammar. I write correctly enough now. O, how I wish school was out !

Lesson 1.2

Prose & Poetry

RHYME SCHEME: AABB

Language Logic

SENTENCE DIAGRAMMING

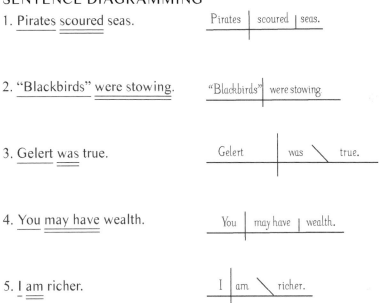

1. Pirates scoured seas.

2. "Blackbirds" were stowing.

3. Gelert was true.

4. You may have wealth.

5. I am richer.

Eloquent Expression

SENTENCE STYLE – SYNONYMS

Gelert was faithful to his duty till his sad demise, and loyalty blent with his dying breath.

Lesson 1.3

Prose & Poetry

RHYMING WORDS

Spelled the Same: *lays – days; tales – Wales; death – breath; things – brings; untold – gold; be – me*

Spelled Differently: *me – sea; teeth – beneath; Ivanhoe – know; touch – such*

Rhyming Words (*Answers may vary*): *stow, blow, dough, though, hoe, woe, whoa*

Language Logic

SENTENCE DIAGRAMMING

1. My <u>mother</u> always <u>read</u> the most magnificent tales.

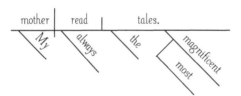

2. <u>Pirates</u> <u>were clenching</u> cutlasses (in their yellow teeth.)

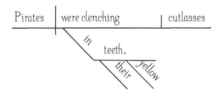

3. <u>You</u> <u>may have</u> tangible wealth untold.

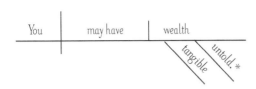

*Untold is actually a participle from the verb *to tell*. If students are familiar with participles and know how to diagram them, they may do so (verbals go on a curved line below the word they modify). At this point, it is fine for students to diagram this like an adjective, since that is its function in the sentence.

4. The hound was true (to his trust.)

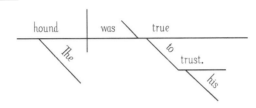

5. Man's extremity is God's opportunity.

Eloquent Expression

COPIA OF WORDS   ANTONYMS

Answers will vary: Gelert was *not disloyal* to his trust, even *unto his* tragic death, and faithfulness blent with his final breath.

Notice that *till his* is also changed to keep the sense of the sentence. Otherwise, it might sound like he became disloyal at his death.

Lesson 1.4

Language Logic

SENTENCE DIAGRAMMING

1. Mother read lays of ancient and gallant and golden days.

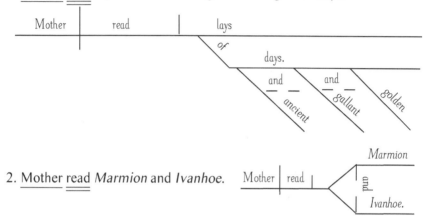

2. Mother read *Marmion* and *Ivanhoe*.

3. I had a Mother; she read (to me.)

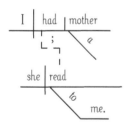

4. Gelert (of Wales) was faithful and true.

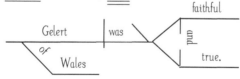

5. Now abideth faith, hope, and charity. —I Corinthians 13:13

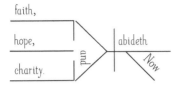

Eloquent Expression

SENTENCE CLASS BY USE

Examples: Declarative, Exclamatory, Interrogative, Imperative

Answers may vary:

Did I have a Mother who read to me? I had a Mother who read to me!

Mother, please read to me.

Lesson 2

❦

THE DESTRUCTION OF SENNACHERIB

The Assyrian came down like the wolf on the fold,
And his cohorts were gleaming in purple and gold;
And the sheen of their spears was like stars on the sea,
When the blue wave rolls nightly on deep Galilee.

Like the leaves of the forest when Summer is green,
That host with their banners at sunset were seen:
Like the leaves of the forest when Autumn hath blown,
That host on the morrow lay withered and strown.

For the Angel of Death spread his wings on the blast,
And breathed in the face of the foe as he passed;
And the eyes of the sleepers waxed deadly and chill,
And their hearts but once heaved, and for ever grew still!

And there lay the steed with his nostril all wide,
But through it there rolled not the breath of his pride;
And the foam of his gasping lay white on the turf,
And cold as the spray of the rock-beating surf.

And there lay the rider distorted and pale,
With the dew on his brow, and the rust on his mail:
And the tents were all silent, the banners alone,
The lances unlifted, the trumpet unblown.

And the widows of Ashur are loud in their wail,
And the idols are broke in the temple of Baal;
And the might of the Gentile, unsmote by the sword,
Hath melted like snow in the glance of the Lord!.

— GEORGE GORDON, LORD BYRON

❦

Lesson 2.1

Prose & Poetry

LITERARY ELEMENTS

3 **Observe the Invention and Arrangement**
- ◆ **Lyrical Elements**
  - The poet gives a vivid description of the army before and after their defeat.
  - He makes us hear the stillness and suddenness of death. He makes us hear the wail of the widows back in the land of Assyria.
  - He makes many comparisons – Sennacherib (the Assyrian) is like a wolf; the spears are as numerous as the stars shining on the sea; the army is as numerous as leaves on trees in the summer forest, and then they are like dead shriveled leaves in late Autumn; etc.

- ◆ **Narrative Elements**
  - **Setting** This is a story from the Bible (II Kings 18-19 and Isaiah 36-37). It is a retelling of a real historical event that took place in Jerusalem during the reign of King Hezekiah, some time around 700 B.C.
  - **Characters** Sennacherib, his army, the Angel of Death, the army's horses, the widows of Asshur.
  - **Conflict** The city is under siege by a mighty army.
  - **Resolution** The problem for those in the besieged city is solved. The Gentile army was wiped out by the Lord without a battle on the part of the besieged.

4 **Investigate the Context**

- ◆ Identify the poem's **Literary Genre**
  - **Genre by literary period** – early 19th century British.

Byron was one of the major Romantic poets. If you wish, you can do some research and describe the period of Romanticism to your students, but this is completely optional.

- **Genre by poetic/narrative category** – narrative

Lesson 2.2

Prose & Poetry

RHYME ANALYSIS
Rhyme Scheme: AABB

Eloquent Expression

COPIA OF WORDS & CONSTRUCTION: DIALOGUE
Answers will vary: "I will come down, " the Assyrian said, "like the wolf on the fold." "I will come down like the wolf on the fold," the Assyrian said.

Lesson 2.3

Prose & Poetry

RHYMING WORDS
Spelled the Same: *fold – gold, green – seen; blown – strown; chill – still; wide – pride; turf – surf; sword – Lord*

Spelled Differently: *sea – Galilee, blast – passed; pale – mail; alone – unblown, wail – Baal*

Rhyming Words (*Answers may vary*): *hail, pail, sail, pale, bale, whale, vale, veil*

Language Logic

PARSING THE NOUN – HARVEY'S EXERCISE 39B

2. Shakespeare lived in Queen Elizabeth's reign. 4. Temperance is a virtue. 7. The little army fought bravely on that day. 8. Where are the Platos and Aristotles of mod ern times?

WORD	PART OF SPEECH	DEFINE	CLASSIFY	PROPERTIES	FUNCTION
2. Shake-speare	noun	person	proper	3rd singular masculine	subject
2. Queen Elizabeth's	noun	person	proper	3rd singular feminine	shows pos-session
2. reign	noun	idea	common	3rd singular neuter	OP *in*
4. temper-ance	noun	idea	common	3rd singular neuter	subject
4. virtue	noun	idea	common	3rd singular neuter	PN *is*
7. army	noun	thing	common	3rd singular neuter	subject
7. day	noun	thing	common	3rd singular common	OP *on*
8. Platos	noun	person	proper	3rd plural masculine	subject
8. Aristotles	noun	person	proper	3rd plural masculine	subject
8. times	noun	thing	common	3rd plural neuter	OP *of*

FORMATION OF PLURAL NOUNS – HARVEY'S EXERCISE 39C (OPTIONAL)

1. I have two brothers-in-law.

2. There were three knights-templar in the procession.

3. Nebulae are sometimes called stardust.

4. I saw the two Mrs. Jacksons.

5. He called at Steeles the banker's.

6. The Joneses were all there.

7. The boy's slate was broken. (could also be boys')

8. The men's wages should be paid promptly.

9. She is reading her sister Susan's book.

10. He studied O. B. Pierce's Grammar.

11. He has octavos, quartos, and folios, among his books.

12. There are three chimneys on that house.

13. We regard them as singular phenomena.

SENTENCE DIAGRAMMING

1. Was that host seen (at sunset?)

2. Angel of Death, spread your wings (on the blast.)

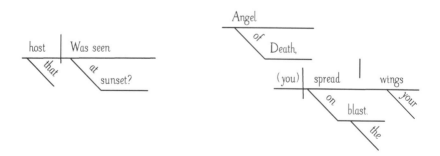

Eloquent Expression

COPIA OF WORDS: DIALOGUE TAGS

Answers will vary: "Richer than I," penned the poet, "you can never be –
I had a mother who read to me." "Richer than I you can never be – I had a
mother who read to me," breathed the poet.

Lesson 2.4

Language Logic

SENTENCE DIAGRAMMING AND PARSING

1. That host (with their banners) (at sunset) were seen.

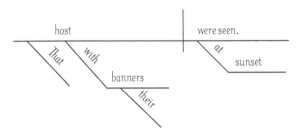

2. The Angel (of Death) spread his wings (in the blast), and breathed (in
the face) (of the foe.)

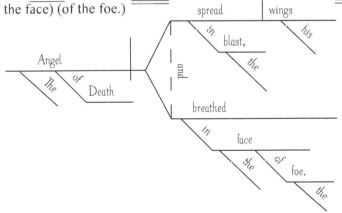

3. Their hearts but once heaved, and forever grew still!

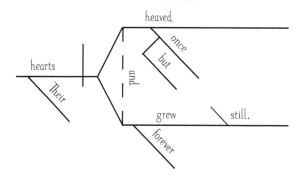

For parsing: OP x = Object of the preposition x; DO x= Direct object of the verb x.

WORD	PART OF SPEECH	DEFINE	CLASSIFY	PROPERTIES	FUNCTION
host (1)	noun	person	common	3rd plural common* (because the poet follows with *were*; modern usage is usually singular)	subject
banners (1)	noun	thing	common	3rd plural neuter	OP *with*
sunset (1)	noun	thing	common	3rd singular neuter	OP *at*
Angel (2)	noun	person	proper	3rd singular masculine (generally)	subject
wings (2)	noun	thing	common	3rd plural neuter	DO *spread*
foe (2)	noun	person	common	3rd singular common	object of preposition *of*
hearts (3)	noun	thing	common	3rd plural neuter	subject

Eloquent Expression

COPIA REVIEW – SYNONYMS

Answers will vary: The strength of the foreigner, unstruck by the blade, hath thawed like ice in the gaze of the Lord.

COPIA REVIEW – ANTONYMS

Answers will vary: And the widows of Ashur are not calm in their wail, and the idols are not unshattered in the temple of Baal.

COPIA REVIEW – SENTENCE CLASS BY USE

Answers may vary: Their hearts but once heaved, and forever grew still. Did their hearts but once heave, and forever grow still? Hearts, but once heave, and forever grow still.

Lesson 3

The Farmer and His Sons
from The Aesop for Children by Milo Winter

A rich old farmer, who felt that he had not many more days to live, called his sons to his bedside. |

"My sons," he said, "heed what I have to say to you. | Do not on any account part with the estate that has belonged to our family for so many generations. | Somewhere on it is hidden a rich treasure. I do not know the exact spot, but it is there, and you will surely find it. | Spare no energy and leave no spot unturned in your search." |

The father died, | and no sooner was he in his grave than the sons set to work digging with all their might, turning up every foot of ground with their spades, and going over the whole farm two or three times. |

No hidden gold did they find; | but at harvest time when they had settled their accounts and had pocketed a rich profit far greater than that of any of their neighbors, | they understood that the treasure their father had told them about was the wealth of a bountiful crop, and that in their industry had they found the treasure. |

Industry is itself a treasure.

Prose & Poetry

LITERARY ELEMENTS

3 Observe the Invention and Arrangement

- **Narrative Elements**

  - **Setting** The story is set on a farm, sometime in the past.

  - **Characters** The farmer and his three sons

  - **Conflict** The dying father has told the sons there is a treasure buried on the farm, and the sons must find it.

  - **Resolution** The sons work very hard, turning the ground over and over, in their quest to find the treasure. In the end, though they do not find a physical hidden treasure, the process of working the soil creates a bountiful crop, and they yield great profit from it.

4 Investigate the Context

- Identify the poem's **Literary Genre**

  - **Genre by literary period** – Ancient Greek

  - **Genre by poetic/narrative category** – fiction

5 Connect the Thoughts

- Stories with similar plots, messages, or characters: Thomas Edison, Pilgrims

- Proverbs or other well-known quotations? "Success is 90% perspiration and 10% inspiration."—Thomas Alva Edison

Lesson 3.2

Prose & Poetry

NARRATIVE PLOT ANALYSIS

The lines inserted in the selection at the beginning of this lesson provide one suggestion for dividing the narrative into a series of actions. Please note that other divisions are possible. Ask your students to give their reasons for their division of the action.

Language Logic

SENTENCE DIAGRAMMING AND PARSING

Spare no energy and leave no spot unturned (in your search.)

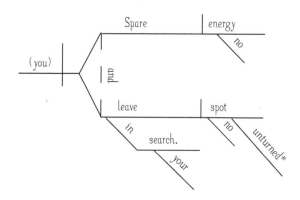

Unturned is a participle from the verb to turn. If students are familiar with participles and know how to diagram them, they may do so (verbals go on a curved line below the word they modify). At this point, however, it is fine for students to diagram this like an adjective, since that is its function in the sentence.

WORD	PART OF SPEECH	DEFINE	CLASSIFY	PROPERTIES	FUNCTION
energy	noun	thing	common	3rd singular neuter	DO *spare*
spot	noun	place	common	3rd singular neuter	DO *leave*

WORD	PART OF SPEECH	DEFINE	CLASSIFY	PROPERTIES	FUNCTION
search	noun	idea	common	3rd singular neuter	OP *in*

Eloquent Expression

COPIA OF WORDS: NOUNS

Answers will vary: 1. farmer – agronomist, rancher, sower, tiller, husbandman 2. treasure – fortune, riches, wealth, cache

COPIA OF WORDS: ADJECTIVES

Answers will vary: 1. farmer – *old, dying, elderly, wise, astute, perceptive* 2. treasure   *true, real, actual, unexpected, unanticipated*

Lesson 3.3

Language Logic

SENTENCE DIAGRAMMING

I do not know the exact spot, but you will surely find it.

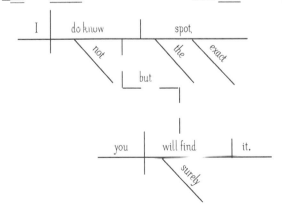

Eloquent Expression

COPIA OF WORDS: VERBS

Answers will vary: 1. called – *summoned, assembled, gathered* 2. find – *discover, dug up, unearth, come upon, recover*

COPIA OF WORDS: ADVERBS

Answers will vary: 1. called – *sadly, wisely, quickly* 2. find – *surely, certainly, eventually, someday*

Lesson 3.4

Eloquent Expression

COPIA REVIEW – DIALOGUE TAGS

Answers will vary: "My sons, heed what I have to say to you," he said. He said, "My sons, heed what I have to say to you."

COPIA REVIEW – SYNONYMS

Answers will vary: The <u>prize</u> was the <u>bounty</u> of a <u>copious</u> harvest which their <u>labor</u> had <u>supplied</u>.

COPIA REVIEW – ANTONYMS

Answers will vary: <u>Do not ignore</u> what I have to say to you.

COPIA REVIEW – SENTENCE CLASS BY USE

Answers may vary: You should heed what I have to say to you. Will you heed what I have to say to you? You should heed what I have to say to you!

Lesson 4

☙

THE FARMER AND HIS SONS

from FABLES OF AESOP & BABRIUS, translated by John Benson Rose

> A Farmer to his sons when near death
> Bequeathed his heritage. "My sons, my breath
> Is fast departing me; my treasures lie
> Amidst the vines—go search there when I die."
> They thought he spoke of treasure buried there,
> And searched and searched thro' the revolving year;
> And autumn came and with it such a vintage
> As was indeed a veritable mintage.
> Then they discovered labor was the treasure
> Which rendered them return in triple measure.

☙

Lesson 4.1

Prose & Poetry

LITERARY ELEMENTS

3 **Observe the Invention and Arrangement**
- ◆ **Lyrical Elements**
    - ▪ Describes the year, the treasure
- ◆ **Narrative Elements** see Lesson 3.1

4 **Investigate the Context**
- ◆ Identify the poem's **Literary Genre**
    - ▪ **Genre by literary period** – early 20th century English translation of ancient Roman poem
    - ▪ **Genre by poetic/narrative category** – narrative

Lesson 4.2

Language Logic

SENTENCE DIAGRAMMING AND PARSING

The sons dug (with all) (of their might), turned up every foot (of ground), and went (over the whole farm.)

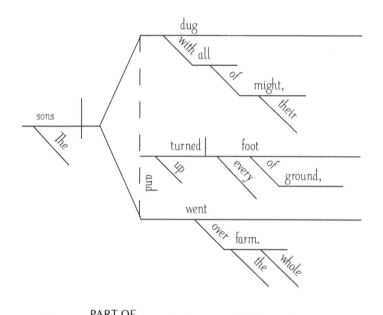

WORD	PART OF SPEECH	DEFINE	CLASSIFY	PROPERTIES	FUNCTION
sons	noun	person	common	3rd plural masculine	subject
might	noun	idea	common	3rd singular neuter	OP *of*
foot	noun	thing	common	3rd singular neuter	DO *turned*
ground	noun	thing	common	3rd singular neuter	OP *of*

Eloquent Expression

COPIA OF CONSTRUCTION: OPENING WORDS

Answers will vary: Turning up every foot of ground, the sons dug with all of their might, and went over the whole farm two or three times. Going over the whole farm two or three times, the sons dug with all of their might and turned up every foot of ground.

Lesson 4.3

Language Logic

SENTENCE DIAGRAMMING AND PARSING

No hidden gold did they find; the treasure was the wealth (of a bountiful crop.)

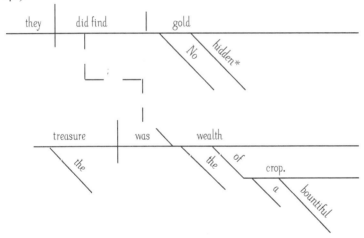

Hidden is a participle from the verb *to hide*. If students are familiar with participles and know how to diagram them, they may do so (verbals go on a curved line below the word they modify). At this point, however, it is fine for students to diagram this like an adjective, since that is its function in the sentence.

WORD	PART OF SPEECH	DEFINE	CLASSIFY	PROPERTIES	FUNCTION
gold	noun	thing	common	3rd singular neuter	DO *find*
treasure	noun	thing	common	3rd singular neuter	subject
wealth	noun	idea	common	3rd singular neuter	PN *was*
crop	noun	thing	common	3rd singular neuter	OP *of*

Lesson 5

❧

THE LAND OF STORY-BOOKS

At evening when the lamp is lit,
Around the fire my parents sit;
They sit at home and talk and sing,
And do not play at anything.

Now, with my little gun, I crawl
All in the dark along the wall,
And follow round the forest track
Away behind the sofa back.

There, in the night, where none can spy,
All in my hunter's camp I lie,
And play at books that I have read
Till it is time to go to bed.

These are the hills, these are the woods,
These are my starry solitudes;
And there the river by whose brink
The roaring lions come to drink.

I see the others far away
As if in firelit camp they lay,
And I, like to an Indian scout,
Around their party prowled about.

So, when my nurse comes in for me,
Home I return across the sea,
And go to bed with backward looks
At my dear land of Story-books.

— ROBERT LOUIS STEVENSON

❧

Lesson 5.1

Prose & Poetry

LITERARY ELEMENTS

3 Observe the Invention and Arrangement
◆ **Lyrical Elements**

- The Land of Story-Books is the imaginary land which the young boy visits each evening when his family gathers around the fire. This land and its inhabitants are inspired by the books he has read.
- Mostly sense of sight — the gun, the boy crawling behind the sofa, the hills, the stars, the woods, etc.
- His imagination is compared to a land. He compares himself to an Indian scout, coming and going from this land so silently that no one hears him or suspects what he is doing, though they are sitting right there with him.

4 Investigate the Context
◆ Identify the poem's **Literary Genre**

- **Genre by literary period** – late 19th century British
- **Genre by poetic/narrative category** – lyrical

Language Logic

SENTENCE DIAGRAMMING AND PARSING

Home I return (across the sea), and go (to bed) (with backward looks) (at my dear land) (of Story-books.)

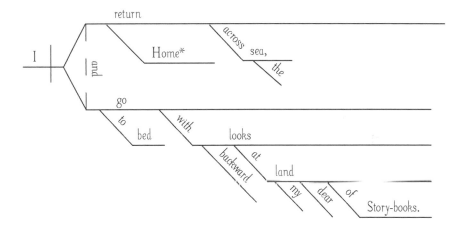

Home is an adverbial noun here. See Sentence Sense – Modifiers: Adverbial Nouns

WORD	PART OF SPEECH	DEFINE	CLASSIFY	PROPERTIES	FUNCTION
looks	noun	idea	common	3rd plural neuter	OP *with*
sea	noun	thing or place	common	3rd singular neuter	OP *across*
Story-books	noun	thing	common	3rd plural neuter	OP *of*

Lesson 5.2

Prose & Poetry

RHYME ANALYSIS
Rhyme Scheme: AABB

Eloquent Expression

COPIA REVIEW: VERBS
Answers will vary: 1. So, when my nurse *too soon arrives* for me, home I *retire regretfully* across the sea.

2. I *journey ruefully* to bed with backward looks at my dear land of Story-books.

Lesson 5.3

Prose & Poetry

RHYMING WORDS
Spelled the Same: *it − sit; sing − anything; track − back; brink − drink; away − lay; scout − about; looks − books.*

Spelled Differently: *crawl − wall; spy − lie; read − bed; woods − solitudes (consonance); me − sea*

Rhyming Words (*Answers may vary*): *drawl, awl, squall, fall, doll, loll, maul, y'all*

Language Logic

PARSING THE PERSONAL PRONOUN – HARVEY'S EXERCISE 65

1. He and I attend the same school. 3. Have you seen him to-day?
6. The wicked is snared in the work of his own hands. 11 . My country, 't is of thee, Sweet land of liberty, Of thee, I sing. 12. Thou great Instructor, lest I stray, Teach thou my erring feet thy way.

WORD	PART OF SPEECH	DEFINE	CLASSIFY	PROPERTIES	FUNCTION
1. he	pronoun	unknown	personal	3rd singular masculine	subject
1. I	pronoun	unknown	personal	1st singular common	subject
3. you	pronoun	unknown	personal	2nd singular or plural	subject
3. him	pronoun	unknown	personal	3rd singular masculine	DO *seen*
6. his	pronoun	*the wicked*	personal	3rd singular masculine	shows possession
11. My	pronoun	the poet	personal	1st singular common	shows possession
11. thee	pronoun	*my country*	personal	2nd singular feminine (usually)	OP *of*
11. I	pronoun	the poet	personal	1st singular common	subject
11. thee	pronoun	*my country*	personal	2nd singular feminine (usually)	OP *of*
12. Thou	pronoun	*God*	personal	2nd singular masculine	direct address

WORD	PART OF SPEECH	DEFINE	CLASSIFY	PROPERTIES	FUNCTION
12. I	pronoun	the poet	personal	1st singular common	subject
12. thou	pronoun	*God*	personal	2nd singular masculine	subject
12. my	pronoun	the poet	personal	1st singular common	shows possession
12. thy	pronoun	*God*	personal	2nd singular masculine	shows possession

SENTENCE DIAGRAMMING

1. Have you seen him today?

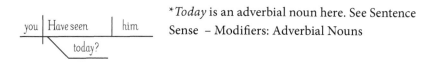

*_Today_ is an adverbial noun here. See Sentence Sense – Modifiers: Adverbial Nouns

2. I saw it (with my own eyes.)

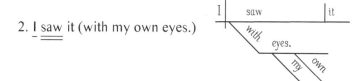

3. The Scot, Robert Louis Stevenson, wrote this poem.

4. Stevenson himself was a sickly child.

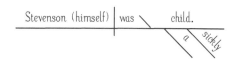

Eloquent Expression

COPIA REVIEW: SYNONYMS

Answers will vary: When my *nanny shows up* for me, *to my house** I *journey* across the *ocean,* and go *to my sleep* with *longing glances* at my *precious province* of *fairy tales.*

*Because *home* is an adverbial noun, any synonym will probably require the addition of a preposition.

COPIA REVIEW: ANTONYMS

Answers will vary: I see the others *not nearby.*

Lesson 5.4

Prose & Poetry

STANZA FORM

"Land of Story-Books" is written in elegiac (heroic) quatrain. This is the stanza form for all the poems we have studied thus far.

Language Logic

PARSING THE POSSESSIVE PRONOUN – HARVEY'S EXERCISE 69

1. The farm is neither his nor theirs. 2. Is that horse of yours lame yet? 4. He is an old friend of ours. 5. This book is not mine; it must be his or hers. 7. Friend of mine, why so sad?

WORD	PART OF SPEECH	DEFINE	CLASSIFY	PROPERTIES	FUNCTION
1. his	pronoun	possessor and thing possessed (*farm*)	possessive	3rd singular masculine	PN renames *farm*
1. theirs	pronoun	possessor and thing possessed (*farm*)	possessive	3rd plural common	PN renames *farm*
2. yours	pronoun	possessor and thing possessed (*horse*)	possessive	2nd singular common (or plural)	OP *of*
4. ours	pronoun	possessor and thing possessed (*friend*)	possessive	1st plural common	OP *of*
5. mine	pronoun	possessor and thing possessed (*book*)	possessive	1st singular common	PN renames *book*
5. his	pronoun	possessor and thing possessed (*book*)	possessive	3rd singular masculine	PN renames *book*
5. hers	pronoun	possessor and thing possessed (*book*)	possessive	3rd singular feminine	PN renames *book*
7. mine	pronoun	possessor and thing possessed (*friend*)	possessive	1st singular common	OP *of*

PARSING THE INTERROGATIVE PRONOUN – HARVEY'S EXERCISE 78

1. Who saw the horse run? 2. Whose house is that on the hill yonder? 5. Which will you have, the large or the small book? 8. What can be more beautiful than that landscape?

WORD	PART OF SPEECH	DEFINE	CLASSIFY	PROPERTIES	FUNCTION
1. Who	pronoun	used to ask a question	interrogative	3rd singular common	subject
2. Whose	pronoun	used to ask a question	interrogatives	3rd singular common	shows possession (modifies *house*)
5. Which	pronoun	used to ask a question	interrogative	3rd singular neuter	DO *will have*
8. What	pronoun	used to ask a question	interrogative	3rd singular neuter	subject

SENTENCE DIAGRAMMING

1. He is an old friend of ours.

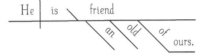

2. This book is not mine; it must be yours or hers.

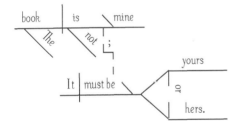

3. Whom did he call?

he | did call? | Whom

Eloquent Expression

COPIA REVIEW – OPENING WORDS

Answers will vary: Home I return across the sea when my nurse comes
in for me, and go to bed with backward looks at my dear land of Story-

books. Across the sea I return home when my nurse comes in for me, and go to bed with backward looks at my dear land of Story-books.

Lesson 5.5

Language Logic

SENTENCE DIAGRAMMING AND PARSING

They sit (at home) and talk and sing, and do not play (at anything.)

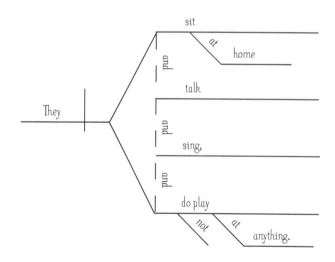

WORD	PART OF SPEECH	DEFINE	CLASSIFY	PROPERTIES	FUNCTION
They	pronoun	stands in for parents	personal	3rd plural common	subject
home	noun	place	common	3rd singular neuter	OP *at*

WORD	PART OF SPEECH	DEFINE	CLASSIFY	PROPERTIES	FUNCTION
anything	noun	thing	common	3rd singular neuter	OP *at*

Eloquent Expression

COPIA REVIEW – SENTENCE CLASS BY USE

Answers will vary: Do I play at books that I have read? Self, play at books that you have read. I play at books that I have read!

COPIA REVIEW – DIALOGUE

Answers will vary: "They sit at home," the poet complained, "and talk and sing, and do not play at anything." "They sit at home and talk and sing," marveled the poet, "and do not play at anything."

Lesson 6

☾

A Book

There is no Frigate like a Book
  To take us Lands away
Nor any Coursers like a Page
  Of prancing Poetry –
This Traverse may the poorest take
  Without oppress of Toll –
How frugal is the Chariot
  That bears the Human Soul –

— EMILY DICKINSON

☾

Lesson 6.1

Prose & Poetry

LITERARY ELEMENTS

3 **Observe the Invention and Arrangement**
  ◆ **Lyrical Elements**

- The poet is describing books, and by extension, reading.

- She makes you "see" images of ships, horses, tollbooths, and chariots.

- She compares a book (reading) to a frigate, coursers (horses), a method of travel, and a chariot.

4 **Investigate the Context** *The rules Dickinson "breaks" are capitalization of words that we would not consider proper nouns (although she might have reason for thinking them so in her context - discuss this idea; A.A. Milne does this same thing in Winnie-the-Pooh as well) and dashes as punctuation where we might expect to see commas or semi-colons or periods. This creates a sense of "running" from thought to thought in the poem.*

 ◆ Identify the poem's **Literary Genre**
  ▪ **Genre by literary period** – 19th century American
  ▪ **Genre by poetic/narrative category** – lyrical

Language Logic

SENTENCE DIAGRAMMING AND PARSING

This Traverse may the poorest take (without oppress) (of Toll.)

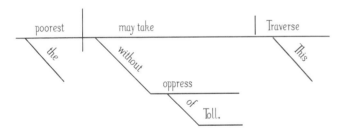

WORD	PART OF SPEECH	DEFINE	CLASSIFY	PROPERTIES	FUNCTION
Traverse	noun	idea	proper*	3rd singular neuter	DO *may take*
oppress	noun	idea	common	3rd singular neuter	OP *without*
Toll	noun	thing	proper*	3rd singular neuter	OP *of*

*We normally classify these nouns as common, but since the poet capitalizes them, she is giving them the particular importance of a proper noun.

Lesson 6.2

Prose & Poetry

RHYME ANALYSIS
Rhyme Scheme: ABCBDEFE
Stanza Form: Octave

Eloquent Expression

COPIA REVIEW: NOUNS
Answers will vary: 1. frigate – (nouns) *ship, vessel, boat;* (adjectives) *frugal, enchanted, imaginary, magical.* 2. traverse – (nouns) *journey, adventure, expedition, passage;* (adjectives) *exciting, frugal, dramatic, delightful*

Lesson 6.3

Prose & Poetry

FIGURES OF SPEECH: SIMILE
Note that all lists of figures in Teaching Helps are meant to be representative, not exhaustive.

"A Book": Frigate like a Book; Coursers like a Page (of prancing Poetry)

A very common and natural mistake in this exercise would be to consider Chariot a simile for a Book. If the words *like, as,* or *than* are not included, it is not a simile, even if a comparison is being made. This is actually an example of **metaphor**, which makes an **indirect** comparison. By definition, a simile must be a **direct** comparison, and thus must include the words *like, as,* or *than.* If it comes up, you can explain this distinction to students. We will cover metaphors later in this book.

"Destruction of Sennacherib": spears like stars; host (with banners) like leaves (of the forsest when Summer...), leaves (of the forest when Autumn...) like host, cold as the spray; might of the Gentile like snow...

You may have to help students rearrange the sentence to see the last two. Also, the words like, as, or than do not always indicate a comparison. If no comparison is made, it is not a simile: He breathed in the face of the foe as he passed. In this case, as is not used to indicate comparison, so this is not a simile.

Language Logic

PARSING THE VERB – HARVEY'S EXERCISE 124

1. They commenced plowing yesterday. 2. I seldom write letters.
3. My father brought me some pine apples when he came from the city. 6. The workmen should have been more careful. 7. Hallowed be Thy name. 10. The weather was unpleasant. 12. Shall I assist you?
15. Remember thy Creator in the days of thy youth.

WORD	PART OF SPEECH	DEFINE	CLASSIFY	PROPERTIES	FUNCTION
1. com-menced	verb	action	transitive	3rd plural past	main verb
2. write	verb	action	transitive	1st singular present	main verb
3. brought	verb	action	transitive	3rd singular past	main verb
3. came	verb	action	intransi-tive	3rd singular past	main verb

WORD	PART OF SPEECH	DEFINE	CLASSIFY	PROPERTIES	FUNCTION
6. should have been	verb	state/ being	linking	3rd plural present perfect	main verb
7. be Hallowed	verb	state/ being	intransi-tive	3rd singular present	main verb
10. was	verb	state/ being	linking	3rd singular past	main verb
12. Shall assist	verb	action	transitive	1st singular future	main verb
15. Remem-ber	verb	action	transitive	2nd singular/ plural pres-ent	main verb

Eloquent Expression

COPIA REVIEW: SYNONYMS

Answers will vary: This journey may a beggar gain, without the care of cost.

COPIA REVIEW: ANTONYMS

Answers will vary: This Traverse may the least wealthy take.

Lesson 6.4

Prose & Poetry

RHYMING WORDS

Spelled the Same: none

Spelled Differently: *away – poetry (slant rhyme), Toll – soul*

Rhyming Words (*Answers may vary*): *troll, droll, stroll, scroll, mole, hole, whole, foal, goal, bowl*

Language Logic

SENTENCE DIAGRAMMING

1. We have named him director.

2. Bring her a book.

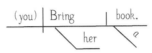

3. God called the light day.

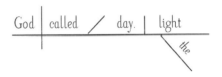

4. Mother read me stories.

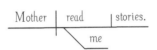

Eloquent Expression

COPIA REVIEW – OPENING WORDS

Answers will vary: The poorest may take this Traverse without oppress of Toll. Without oppress of Toll, this Traverse may the poorest take.

Lesson 6.5

Language Logic

SENTENCE DIAGRAMMING AND PARSING

The poet calls Books "Frigates" and Pages (of Poetry) "Coursers."

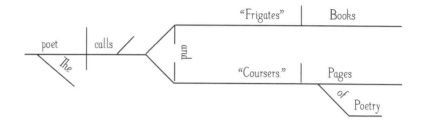

WORD	PART OF SPEECH	DEFINE	CLASSIFY	PROPERTIES	FUNCTION
poet	noun	person	common	3rd singular feminine	subject
calls	verb	action	transitive	3rd singular present	main verb
Books	noun	thing	proper*	3rd plural neuter	DO *calls*
"Frigates"	noun	thing	proper*	3rd plural neuter (or feminine – ships)	OC
Poetry	noun	idea	proper*	3rd singular neuter	OP *of*
"Coursers"	noun	thing	proper*	3rd plural common	OC

*We normally classify these nouns as common, but since the poet capitalizes them, she is giving them the particular importance of a proper noun.

Eloquent Expression

COPIA REVIEW – SENTENCE CLASS BY USE

Answers will vary: This chariot does bear the human soul frugally. Does not this Chariot bear the Human Soul frugally? Chariot, bear the human soul frugally.

COPIA REVIEW – DIALOGUE

Answers will vary: "There is no frigate," Emily Dickinson mused, "like a book." "There is no frigate like a book," Emily Dickinson wrote.

Lesson 7

❦

Bruce and the Spider

from Fifty Famous Stories Retold by James Baldwin

[Prologue] There was once a king of Scotland whose name was Robert Bruce. He had need to be both brave and wise, for the times in which he lived were wild and rude. The King of England was at war with him, and had led a great army into Scotland to drive him out of the land.

[Beginning] Battle after battle had been fought. Six times had Bruce led his brave little army against his foes; and six times had his men been beaten, and driven into flight. At last his army was scattered, and he was forced to hide himself in the woods and in lonely places among the mountains.

One rainy day, Bruce lay on the ground under a rude shed, listening to the patter of the drops on the roof above him. He was tired and sick at heart, and ready to give up all hope. It seemed to him that there was no use for him to try to do anything more.

As he lay thinking, he saw a spider over his head, making ready to weave her web. He watched her as she toiled slowly and with great care. Six times she tried to throw her frail thread from one beam to another, and six times it fell short.

"Poor thing!" said Bruce: "you, too, know what it is to fail."

But the spider did not lose hope with the sixth failure. With still more care, she made ready to try for the seventh time. Bruce almost forgot his own troubles as he watched her swing herself out upon the slender line. Would she fail again? No! The thread was carried safely to the beam, and fastened there.

"I, too, will try a seventh time!" cried Bruce.

He arose and called his men together. He told them of his plans, and sent them out with messages of cheer to his disheartened people. Soon there was an army of brave Scotchmen around him. Another battle was fought, and the King of England was glad to go back into his own country. [End]

[Epilogue] I have heard it said, that, after that day, no one by the name of Bruce would ever hurt a spider. The lesson which the little creature had taught the king was never forgotten.

Lesson 7.1

Prose & Poetry

LITERARY ELEMENTS

3 Observe the Invention and Arrangement

◆ **Lyrical Elements**

- Describes
- Senses
- Comparisons

◆ **Narrative Elements**

- **Setting** Scotland, early fourteenth century. (Battle of Bannockburn was June 24, 1314.)
- **Characters** Robert the Bruce and a spider
- **Conflict** Bruce is discouraged because his army is defeated and scattered. A spider is spinning her web, attempting to attach thread to a beam just out of reach.
- **Resolution** Spider is successful on her seventh attempt; Bruce is encouraged to try again by her determination.

4 Investigate the Context

◆ Identify the poem's **Literary Genre**

- **Genre by literary period** – early 20th century American retelling of a story from fourteenth century Scotland

■ **Genre by poetic/narrative category** – Treat as non-fiction, with possible fictional details: Robert Bruce is considered a national hero in Scotland, as is George Washington in the United States. This story is a part of the "mythology" of the Scottish nation, very much like the American story of George Washington and his hatchet. The word "mythology " does not imply that any of these stories are necessarily false. By "mythology," we are referring to the accepted narrative of a particular nation which helps to shape and express its values. This is related to Tolkien's idea that myth is often the best way to convey truth that would not otherwise be expressed. (*The Inklings*, by Humphrey Carpenter, relates a conversation about this between Tolkien and his then-athiest friend, C.S. Lewis.)

5 Connect the Thoughts

◆ The Crow and the Pitcher," Aesop (perseverance); George Washington "myths" – cherry tree incident, penny across the river

◆ "'Tis a lesson you should heed: Try, try again. If at first you don't succeed, Try, try again." —folk proverb popularized by William Hickson, 1836; "I have not failed. I've just found 10,000 ways that won't work." —Thomas Edison

---

Lesson 7.2

Language Logic

SENTENCE DIAGRAMMING AND PARSING

He had need (of both bravery and wisdom), for the times were wild and rude.

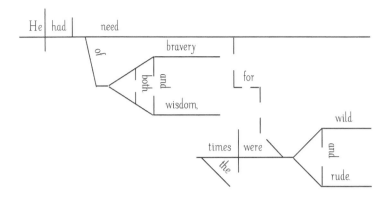

WORD	PART OF SPEECH	DEFINE	CLASSIFY	PROPERTIES	FUNCTION
He	pronoun	stands in for *Bruce*	personal	3rd singular masculine	subject of principal clause
had need	verb	action	transitive	3rd singular past	main verb of 1st principal clause
wisdom	noun	idea	common	3rd singular neuter (or feminine)	OP *of*
times	noun	idea	common	3rd plural neuter	subject of 2nd principal clause

Eloquent Expression

COPIA OF WORDS: NOUN CLASS

Answers will vary: 1. Edward I of England opposed Robert Bruce of Scotland during the Scottish War for Independence. 2. The brave army fought the Battle of Bannockburn, and the enemy (king, leader, etc) returned to England.

COPIA OF WORDS: NOUN AND PRONOUN PROPERTY – NUMBER

Answers will vary: 3. Bruce led his men against his foe (the enemy); now they were hiding in a wood (in the forest). 4. The spiders carry their threads and fasten them on the beams overhead.

COPIA OF WORDS: NOUN AND PRONOUN SWITCH

Answers will vary: 5. He was at war with Robert Bruce, and had led them into Scotland. 6. Bruce watched the spider as she toiled. Six times she tried to throw it.

Lesson 7.3

Prose & Poetry

NARRATIVE PLOT ANALYSIS

This is only a guide to how a student might apply Theon's Six to a narrative. There are no "right" answers. Please work with your students, and allow them to give you the reasons for their answers. Only correct them if absolutely necessary (for example, if they did not do a complete job).

Person

Robert the Bruce – defeated, separated from scattered army, tired, sick at heart, ready to give up hope; Spider – careful and patient

Action

Bruce watched the spider spin her web, and make six unsuccessful attempts to attach it to a beam. She was successful on the seventh try, which gave him hope to try again with his own army.

Place

mountains of Scotland, under a rude shed

Time

after sixth defeat of his army by the King of England.

Manner

Bruce — watched in discouragement at first, in hope at the end; Spider — weaved slowly and with great care

Cause

Bruce — watching because of the rain and his dejection; Spider — because of instinct

Language Logic

SENTENCE DIAGRAMMING AND PARSING

His army was scattered, and Bruce hid himself (in the woods) and (in lonely places) (among the mountains.)

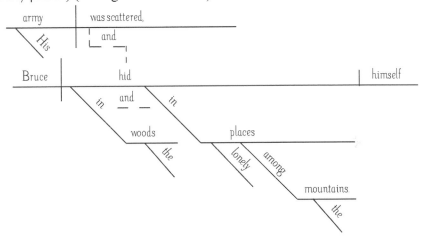

WORD	PART OF SPEECH	DEFINE	CLASSIFY	PROPERTIES	FUNCTION
His	pronoun	stands in for *Bruce*	personal	3rd singular masculine	modifies *army* – shows possession
was scattered	verb	action	intransitive	3rd singular past	main verb of 1st principal clause
Bruce	noun	person	proper	3rd singular masculine	subject of 2nd principal clause
himself	pronoun	stands in for *Bruce*	personal	3rd singular masculine	DO *hid*
mountains	noun	place	common	3rd plural neuter	OP *among*

Eloquent Expression

COPIA OF WORDS: NOUN PROPERTY – PERSON

Answers will vary: 1. I had led the army against my foes, but now I was hiding in the woods. You had led the army against your foes, but now you were hiding in the woods. 2. You, too, will try a seventh time! He, too, will try a seventh time

COPIA OF WORDS: VERB PROPERTY – TENSE

Answers will vary: 3. The king of England opposes the king of Scotland in the war. The king of England will oppose the king of Scotland in the war. The king of England has opposed the king of Scotland in the war. The king of England had opposed the king of Scotland in the war. The king of England will have opposed the king of Scotland in the war. 4. Six times the spider tries to throw her thread. Six times the spider will try to throw her thread. Six times the spider has tried to throw her thread. Six times the spider had tried to throw her thread. Six times the spider will have tried to throw her thread.

Lesson 7.4

Eloquent Expression

COPIA OF WORDS: APPOSITIVES

Answers will vary: 3. Robert Bruce, the King of Scotland, had need to be both brave and wise. 4. The King of England, Edward I, was glad to go back into his own country, England.

COPIA OF WORDS: POSSESSIVES

Answers will vary: 1. Six times the thread of the spider fell short, but the seventh, her effort succeeded. 2. The spider's lesson was never forgotten by the family of Bruce.

Eloquent Expression

LITERARY IMITATION

Peter was most dreadfully frightened; he rushed all (over the garden), for he had forgotten the way (to the gate.)

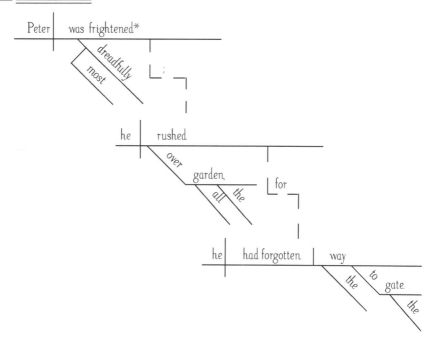

You could also reasonably call was *a linking verb and* frightened *a predicate adjective. Generally compound verbs in English are diagrammed together as the verb phrase, so if students makes this argument, they should be commended for good critical thinking!*

Lesson 8

❦

BRUCE AND THE SPIDER

from TALES OF A SCOTTISH GRANDFATHER by Sir Walter Scott

It was about this time that an incident took place, which, although it rests only on tradition in families of the name of Bruce, is rendered probable by the manners of the times. After receiving the last unpleasing intelligence from Scotland, Bruce was lying one morning on his wretched bed, and deliberating with himself whether he had not better resign all thoughts of again attempting to make good his right to the Scottish crown, and, dismissing his followers, transport himself and his brothers to the Holy Land, and spend the rest of his life fighting against the Saracens; by which he thought, perhaps, he might deserve the forgiveness of Heaven for the great sin of stabbing Comyn in the church in Dumfries. But then, on the other hand, he thought it would be both criminal and cowardly to give up his attempts to restore freedom to Scotland, while there yet remained the least chance of his being successful in an undertaking, which, rightly considered, was much more his duty than to drive the infidels out of Palestine, though the superstition of his age might think otherwise.

While he was divided betwixt these two reflections, and doubtful of what he should do, Bruce was looking upward to the roof of the cabin in which he lay; and his eye was attracted by a spider, which, hanging at the end of a long thread of its own spinning, was endeavouring, as is the fashion of that creature, to swing itself from one beam in the roof to another, for the purpose of fixing the line on which it meant to stretch its web. The insect made the attempt again and again without success; and at length Bruce counted that it had tried to carry its point six times, and been as often unable to do so. It came into his head that he himself fought just six battles against the English and their allies, and that the poor persevering spider was exactly in the same situation with himself, having made as many trials, and been as often disappointed in what it aimed at. "Now," thought Bruce, " as I have no means of knowing what is best to be done, I will be guided by the luck which shall attend this spider. If the insect shall make another effort to fix its thread, and shall be successful, I will venture a seventh time to try my fortune in Scotland; but if the spider shall fail I will go to the wars in Palestine, and never return to my native country more."

While Bruce was forming this resolution, the spider made another exertion with all the force it could muster, and fairly succeeded in fastening its thread to the beam which it had so often in vain attempted to reach. Bruce, seeing the success of the spider, resolved to try his own fortune; and as he had never before gained a victory, so he never afterwards sustained any considerable check or defeat. I have often met with people of the name Bruce, so completely persuaded of the truth of this story, that they would not on any account kill a spider; because it was that insect which had shown the example of perseverance, and given a signal of good luck, to their great namesake.

CR

Lesson 8.1

Prose & Poetry

LITERARY ELEMENTS

4 **Investigate the Context**
  ◆ Identify the poem's **Literary Genre**
    ▪ **Genre by literary period** – Nineteenth century Scottish
    ▪ **Genre by poetic/narrative category** – see Lesson 7.1

Lesson 8.2

Language Logic

SENTENCE DIAGRAMMING AND PARSING

(On a rainy day,) Bruce <u>lay</u> (on the ground) (under a rude shed) and
<u>listened</u> (to the patter) (of the drops) (on the roof) (above him.)

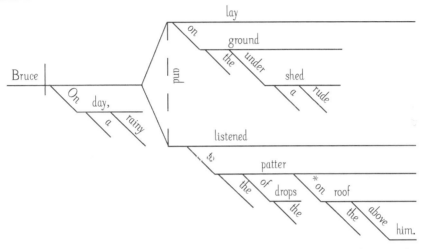

Depending on how you think about it, on the roof *could also modify* drops. *Ask
students to give their reasoning, but accept either answer.*

WORD	PART OF SPEECH	DEFINE	CLASSIFY	PROPERTIES	FUNCTION
day	noun	idea	common	3rd singular neuter	OP *on*
lay	verb	state/ being	intransi- tive	3rd singular past	compound main verb of princi- pal clause
listened	verb	action	transitive	3rd singular past	compound main verb of princi- pal clause
drops	noun	thing	common	3rd plural neuter	OP *of*

WORD	PART OF SPEECH	DEFINE	CLASSIFY	PROPERTIES	FUNCTION
him	pronoun	stands in for *Bruce*	personal	3rd singular masculine	OP *above*

Lesson 8.3

Language Logic

SENTENCE DIAGRAMMING AND PARSING

(After that day,) no <u>one</u> (by the name) (of Bruce) <u>would</u> ever <u>hurt</u> a spi-der. The little creature's <u>lesson</u> <u>was</u> never <u>forgotten</u>.

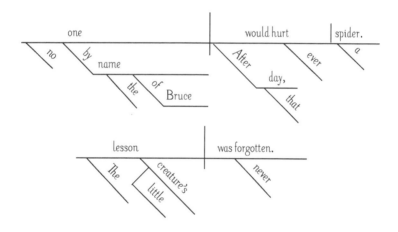

WORD	PART OF SPEECH	DEFINE	CLASSIFY	PROPERTIES	FUNCTION
name	noun	idea	common	3rd singular neuter	OP *by*
Bruce	noun	person	proper	3rd singular masculine	OP *of*

WORD	PART OF SPEECH	DEFINE	CLASSIFY	PROPERTIES	FUNCTION
would hurt	verb	action	transitive	3rd singular past	main verb of principal clause
creature's	noun	thing	common	3rd singular feminine	modifies *lesson*; shows possession

Lesson 9

ᐒ

OCTOBER'S PARTY

October gave a party;
  The leaves by hundreds came —
The Chestnuts, Oaks, and Maples,
  And leaves of every name.

The Sunshine spread a carpet,
  And everything was grand,
Miss Weather led the dancing,
  Professor Wind the band.

The Chestnuts came in yellow,
  The Oaks in crimson dressed;
The lovely Misses Maple
  In scarlet looked their best;

All balanced to their partners,
  And gaily fluttered by;
The sight was like a rainbow
  New fallen from the sky.

Then, in the rustic hollow,
  At hide-and-seek they played;
The party closed at sundown,
  And everybody stayed.

Professor Wind played louder;
  They flew along the ground;
And then the party ended
  In jolly "hands around."

— GEORGE COOPER

ᐒ

Lesson 9.1

Prose & Poetry

LITERARY ELEMENTS

3 Observe the Invention and Arrangement
◆ **Lyrical Elements**

- He describes Autumn leaves falling to the ground and blowing around in the wind.
- He makes you "see" trees and leaves in all their autumn splendor.
- *He compares the leaves to dancers, and the wind to a band leader.*

4 Investigate the Context
◆ Identify the poem's **Literary Genre**

- **Genre by literary period** – 20th century American
- **Genre by poetic/narrative category** – lyrical

Language Logic

SENTENCE DIAGRAMMING AND PARSING
Then, (in the rustic hollow,)

    (At hide-and-seek) they played;

The party closed (at sundown,)

    And everybody stayed.

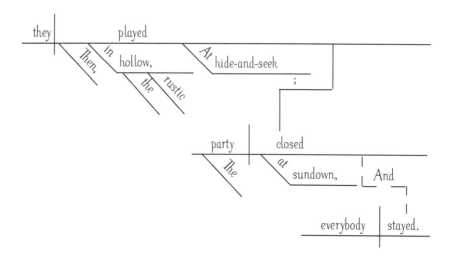

WORD	PART OF SPEECH	DEFINE	CLASSIFY	PROPERTIES	FUNCTION
hollow	noun	place	common	3rd singular neuter	OP *in*
hide-and-seek	noun	thing	proper (names a particular game)	3rd singular neuter	OP *at*
they	pronoun	stands in for *leaves*	personal	3rd plural neuter	subject of principal clause
played	verb	action	intransitive	3rd plural past	main verb of principal clause

Lesson 9.2

Prose & Poetry

SCANSION AND ANALYSIS

Rhyme Scheme: ABCB

Stanza Name: Quatrain

Poetic Meter: Iambic Trimeter

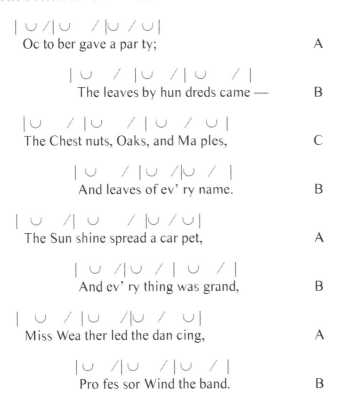

Oc to ber gave a par ty;		A
The leaves by hun dreds came —		B
The Chest nuts, Oaks, and Ma ples,		C
And leaves of ev' ry name.		B
The Sun shine spread a car pet,		A
And ev' ry thing was grand,		B
Miss Wea ther led the dan cing,		A
Pro fes sor Wind the band.		B

Other Iambic Poems: "The Land of Story-Books" is iambic tetrameter. "A Book" is iambic; its lines alternate between tetrameter and trimeter.

Language Logic

PARSING THE ADJECTIVE – HARVEY'S EXERCISE 55

2. Fearful storms sweep over these beautiful islands. 5. I feel sad and lonely. 10. Both horses are lame. 26. With many a weary step, and many a groan, Up the high hill he heaves a huge round stone. — Pope.

WORD	PART OF SPEECH	DEFINE	CLASSIFY	PROPERTIES	FUNCTION
2. fearful	adjective	modifies a noun	descriptive	--	modifies *storm*
2. these	adjective	modifies a noun	definitive	--	modifies *islands*
2. beautiful	adjective	modifies a noun	descriptive	--	modifies *islands*
5. sad	adjective	modifies a pronoun	descriptive	--	PA, modifies *I*
5. lonely	adjective	modifies a pronoun	descriptive	--	PA, modifies *I*
10. both	adjective	modifies a noun	definitive	--	modifies *horses*
10. lame	adjective	modifies a noun	descriptive	--	PA, modifies *horses*
26. many	adjective	modifies a noun	definitive	--	modifies *step*
26. a	adjective	modifies a noun	definitive	--	modifies *step*
26. weary	adjective	modifies a noun	descriptive	--	modifies *step*

WORD	PART OF SPEECH	DEFINE	CLASSIFY	PROPERTIES	FUNCTION
26. many	adjective	modifies a noun	definitive	--	modifies *groan*
26. a	adjective	modifies a noun	definitive	--	modifies *groan*
26. high	adjective	modifies a noun	descriptive	--	modifies *hill*
26. a	adjective	modifies a noun	definitive	--	modifies *stone*
26. huge	adjective	modifies a noun	descriptive	--	modifies *stone*
26. round	adjective	modifies a noun	descriptive	--	modifies *stone*

Lesson 9.3

Prose & Poetry

SCANSION:

| ∪ / | ∪ / | ∪ / ∪ |
The Chest nuts came in yel low,

| ∪ / |∪ / | ∪ / |
The Oaks in crim son dressed;

| ∪ / |∪ / |∪ / ∪ |
The love ly Miss es Ma ple

| ∪ / |∪ / | ∪ / |
In scar let looked their best;

| ∪ / | ∪ / | ∪ / ∪ |
All bal anced to their part ners,

| ∪ / |∪ / | ∪ / |
And gai ly flut tered by;

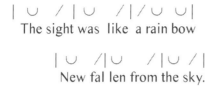

The sight was like a rain bow

New fal len from the sky.

Language Logic

PARSING THE ADVERB – HARVEY'S EXERCISE 132

4. How rapidly the moments fly! 5. He signed it then and there.
11. They were agreeably disap pointed. 16. I have not seen him
since I' returned from New York. 17. Doubtless, ye are the people.

WORD	PART OF SPEECH	DEFINE	CLASSIFY	PROPERTIES	FUNCTION
4. How	adverb	modifies an adverb	--	--	modifies *rapidly*
4. rapidly	adverb	modifies a verb	--	--	modifies *fly*
5. then	adverb	modifies a verb	--	--	modifies *signed*
5. there	adverb	modifies a verb	--	--	modifies *signed*
11. agree-ably	adverb	modifies an adjec-tive	--	--	modifies *disap-pointed*
16. not	adverb	modifies a verb	--	--	modifies *seen*
16. since	adverb	modifies a verb	--	--	modifies *returned*
17. Doubt-less	adverb	modifies a verb	--	--	modifies *are*

Eloquent Expression

FIGURES OF SPEECH: PERSONIFICATION
Representative, not exhaustive.

Personification in "October's Party": October gave a party, leaves come, Sunshine spread carpet, Miss Weather led dancing, Professor Wind (led) the band, Chestnuts came, Oaks in crimson dressed, lovely Misses Maple...looked their best, All balanced to their partners, At hide-and-seek they played, Professor Wind played, They flew.

Personification in "The Reading Mother": Gelert – faithful and true; stories stir; Personification in "The Destruction of Sennarcherib": Angel of Death, steed – pride; trumpets silent; Personification in "The Land of Story-Books": none; Personification in "A Book": prancing poetry; frugal Chariot; Human Soul "borne" in a chariot

Simile in "October's Party": The sight was like a rainbow New fallen from the sky.

Lesson 9.4

Prose & Poetry

SCANSION:

| ∪ /|∪ /|∪ / ∪|
Then, in the rus tic hol low,

|∪ /|∪ /| ∪ / |
At hide-and-seek they played;

|∪ /|∪ / |∪ / ∪|
The par ty closed at sun down,

| ∪ /|∪ /|∪ / |
And ev' ry bod y stayed.

| ∪ ⁄|∪ ⁄ | ∪   ⁄ ∪|
Pro fes sor Wind played loud er;

| ∪   ⁄|∪ ⁄ |∪   ⁄ |
They flew a long the ground;

| ∪ ⁄ | ∪ ⁄|∪ ⁄ ∪|
And then the par ty end ed

|∪ ⁄|∪   ⁄ |∪ ⁄ |
In jol ly "hands a round."

Language Logic

THE PREPOSITION – HARVEY'S EXERCISE 139

1. Will you go with me into the garden? 2. In my Father's house are many mansions. 3. We went over the river, through the corn-fields, into the woods yonder. 5. All came but Mary. 10. Night, sable goddess! from her ebon throne, In ray less majesty, now stretches forth Her leaden scepter o'er a slumbering world.

WORD	PART OF SPEECH	DEFINE	CLASSIFY	PROPERTIES	FUNCTION
1. with	preposi-tion	relates *me* to *go*	--	--	adverbial, modifies *go*
1. into	preposi-tion	relates *garden* to *go*	--	--	adverbial, modifies *go*
2. In	preposi-tion	relates *house* to *mansions*	--	--	adjectival, modifies *mansions*
3. over	preposi-tion	relates *river* to *went*	--	--	adverbial, modifies *went*

WORD	PART OF SPEECH	DEFINE	CLASSIFY	PROPERTIES	FUNCTION
3. through	preposi-tion	relates *corn-fields* to *went*	--	--	adverbial, modifies *went*
3. into	preposi-tion	relates *woods* to *went*	--	--	adverbial, modifies *went*
5. but	preposi-tion	relates *Mary* to *all*	--	--	adjectival, modifies *all*
10. from	preposi-tion	relates *throne* to *stretches*	--	--	adverbial, modifies *stretches*
10. In	preposi-tion	relates *majesty* to *stretches*	--	--	adverbial, modifies *stretches*
10. o' er	preposi-tion	relates *world* to *stretches*	--	--	adverbial, modifies *stretches*

Eloquent Expression

LITERARY IMITATION

The Queen-Mother went quietly (into the bedroom), took all the bed-clothes (off the bed), and put three little peas (on the bedstead.)

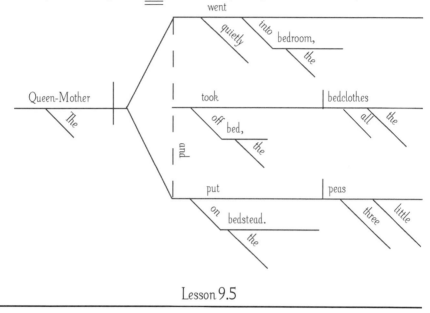

Lesson 9.5

LANGUAGE LOGIC

SENTENCE DIAGRAMMING AND PARSING

Professor Wind played louder;

      They flew (along the ground;)

And then the party ended

      (In jolly "hands around.")

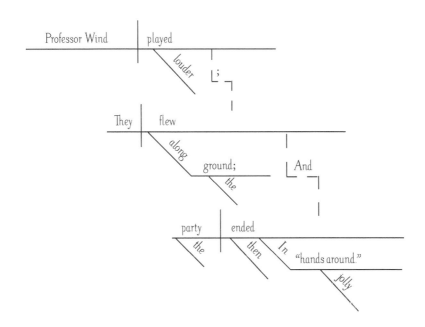

WORD	PART OF SPEECH	DEFINE	CLASSIFY	PROPERTIES	FUNCTION
played	verb	action	intransi-tive	3rd singular past	main verb of princi-pal clause
louder	adverb	modifies verb	--	--	modifies *played*
along the ground	prepo-sitional phrase	connects *ground to flew*	--	--	adverbial, modifies *flew*
then	adverb	modifies verb	--	--	modifies *ended*
jolly	adjective	modifies a noun	descriptive	--	modifies "*hands around*"
"hands around"	noun	thing	proper (names a particular game)	3rd singular	OP *in*

Lesson 10

❧

HIAWATHA

At the door on summer evenings
Sat the little Hiawatha;
Heard the whispering of the pine-trees,
Heard the lapping of the waters,
Sounds of music, words of wonder;
'Minne-wawa!" said the pine-trees,
Mudway-aushka!" said the water.
  Saw the fire-fly, Wah-wah-taysee,
Flitting through the dusk of evening,
With the twinkle of its candle
Lighting up the brakes and bushes,
And he sang the song of children,
Sang the song Nokomis taught him:
"Wah-wah-taysee, little fire-fly,
Little, flitting, white-fire insect,
Little, dancing, white-fire creature,
Light me with your little candle,
Ere upon my bed I lay me,
Ere in sleep I close my eyelids!"
  Saw the moon rise from the water
Rippling, rounding from the water,
Saw the flecks and shadows on it,
Whispered, "What is that, Nokomis?"
And the good Nokomis answered:
"Once a warrior, very angry,
Seized his grandmother, and threw her
Up into the sky at midnight;
Right against the moon he threw her;
'T is her body that you see there."
  Saw the rainbow in the heaven,
In the eastern sky, the rainbow,

Whispered, "What is that, Nokomis?"
And the good Nokomis answered:
"'T is the heaven of flowers you see there;
All the wild-flowers of the forest,
All the lilies of the prairie,
When on earth they fade and perish,
Blossom in that heaven above us."

— HENRY WADSWORTH LONGFELLOW

☙

Lesson 10.1

Prose & Poetry

LITERARY ELEMENTS

3 Observe the Invention and Arrangement
◆ **Lyrical Elements**

- Sounds and sights on a summer evening, in the midnight, and after a rain.
- He makes you "hear" and "see" the natural world through a small boy's eyes, and through the explanations the boy's grandmother gives for the things he sees.
- He compares the actions and sounds of inanimate objects like trees and water to the sounds made by humans or animals.

Investigate the Context
◆ Identify the poem's **Literary Genre**
- **Genre by literary period** – 19th century American
- **Genre by poetic/narrative category** – this selection is lyrical, although the larger poem is narrative (even epic)

Language Logic

SENTENCE DIAGRAMMING AND PARSING

"Once a warrior, very angry,
Seized his grandmother, and threw her
Up (into the sky) (at midnight);

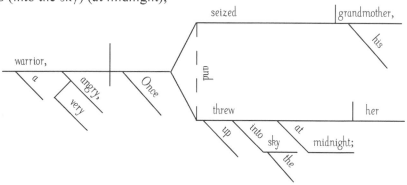

WORD	PART OF SPEECH	DEFINE	CLASSIFY	PROPERTIES	FUNCTION
Once	adverb	modifies a verb	--	--	modifies *threw*
warrior	noun	person	common	3rd singular masculine	subject of principal clause
very	adverb	modifies an adjective	--	--	modifies *angry*
angry	adjective	modifies a noun	descriptive	--	modifies *warrior*
seized	verb	action	transitive	3rd singular past	main verb of principal clause
her	pronoun	stands in for *grandmother*	personal	3rd singular feminine	DO *threw*
into the sky	prepositional phrase	relates *sky* to *threw*	--	--	adverbial, modifies *threw*

WORD	PART OF SPEECH	DEFINE	CLASSIFY	PROPERTIES	FUNCTION
at midnight	prepositional phrase	relates *midnight* to *threw*	--	--	adverbial, modifies *threw*

Lesson 10.2

Prose & Poetry

SCANSION AND ANALYSIS

Rhyme Scheme: blank verse

Stanza Name: n/a

Poetic Meter: Trochaic Tetrameter

| / ∪ | / ∪ | / ∪ | / ∪ |
At the door on sum mer ev' nings

| / ∪ | / ∪ | / ∪ | / ∪ |
Sat the lit tle Hi a wath a;

| / ∪ | / ∪ | / ∪ | / ∪ |
Heard the whisp' ring of the pine-trees,

| / ∪ | / ∪ | / ∪ | / ∪ |
Heard the lap ping of the wa ters,

| / ∪ | / ∪ | / ∪ | / ∪ |
Sounds of mu sic, words of won der;

| / ∪ | / ∪ | / ∪ | / ∪ |
'Min ne-wa wa!" said the pine-trees,

| / ∪ | / ∪ | / ∪ | / ∪ |
Mud way-aush ka!" said the wa ter.

| / ∪ | / ∪ | / ∪ | / ∪ |
Saw the fire-fly, Wah-wah-tay see,

| / ∪| /   ∪| / ∪| / ∪ |
Flit ting through the dusk of ev' ning,

| /   ∪| / ∪| /∪| / ∪ |
With the twin kle of its can dle

| /   ∪| /∪| /   ∪| / ∪ |
Light ing up the brakes and bush es,

| / ∪| / ∪ | / ∪| / ∪ |
And he sang the song of child ren,

| /   ∪| / ∪| / ∪| /   ∪ |
Sang the song No ko mis taught him:

Other Trochaic Poems: This is the first trochaic poem students have encountered in *Bards & Poets II.*

Language Logic

VERBALS: THE PARTICIPLE

1. Here it comes sparkling, and there it lies darkling. 2. The boy passed on, whistling a tune. 3. The fort, situated on a high hill, was captured at daybreak.

Nota Bene: The tendency with participles is to think that they modify verbs, but by definition, a participle is adjectival, and therefore must modify a noun or pronoun.

WORD	PART OF SPEECH	DEFINE	CLASSIFY	PROPERTIES	FUNCTION
1. sparkling	verbal	*to sparkle*	participle	present	modifies *it*
1. darkling	verbal	*to darkle*	participle	present	modifies *it*

WORD	PART OF SPEECH	DEFINE	CLASSIFY	PROPERTIES	FUNCTION
2. whistling	verbal	*to whistle*	participle	present	modifies boy
3. situated	verbal	*to situate*	participle	perfect	modifies fort

1. Here it comes sparkling, and there it lies darkling.

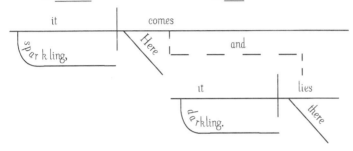

2. The boy passed on, whistling a tune.

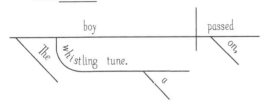

3. The fort, situated on a high hill, was captured at daybreak.

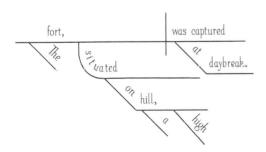

Lesson 10.3

Prose & Poetry

SCANSION:

| ／ ∪| ／ ∪|／∪|／∪ |
"Wah-wah-tay see, lit tle fire-fly,

|／∪|／∪| ／ ∪|／∪ |
Lit tle, flit ting, white-fire in sect,

|／∪| ／ ∪ | ／ ∪ | ／ ∪ |
Lit tle, dan cing, white-fire crea ture,

| ／ ∪| ／ ∪ |／∪|／ ∪ |
Light me with your lit tle can dle,

|／∪|／∪| /∪| ／∪|
Ere up on my bed I lay me,

|／∪|／∪| ／ ∪ |／∪ |
Ere in sleep I   close my eye lids!"

| ／ ∪| ／ ∪| ／ ∪|／∪ |
Saw the moon rise from the wa ter

|／ ∪ | ／ ∪| ／ ∪|／ ∪ |
Rip pling, round ing from the wa ter,

|／ ∪| ／ ∪| ／ ∪|／∪ |
Saw the flecks and shad ows on it,

| ／ ∪ | ／ ∪|／ ∪|／ ∪ |
Whisp ered, "What is that, No ko mis?"

|／ ∪|／ ∪|／∪|／ ∪ |
And the good No ko mis an swered:

| ／ ∪| ／ ∪| ／∪| ／∪ |
"Once a war rior, ve ry ang ry,

| / ∪| / ∪ | / ∪| / ∪ |
Seized his grand moth er, and threw her

|/ ∪| / ∪| / ∪| / ∪ |
Up in to the sky at mid night;

Language Logic

VERBALS: THE GERUND

1. He was (in danger) (of losing his life). 2. The two men commenced searching (for a shelter.) 3. Seeing is believing.

WORD	PART OF SPEECH	DEFINE	CLASSIFY	PROPERTIES	FUNCTION
1. losing	verbal	*to lose*	gerund	present	OP *of*
2. searching	verbal	*to search*	gerund	present	DO *commenced*
3. Seeing	verbal	*to see*	gerund	present	Subject of principal clause
3. believing	verbal	*to believe*	gerund	present	*PN*

1. He was (in danger) (of losing his life.)

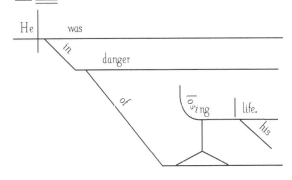

2. The two <u>men</u> <u>commenced</u> searching (for a shelter.)

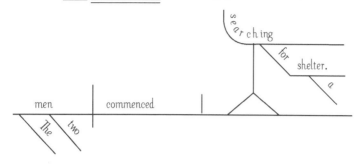

3. <u>Seeing</u> <u>is</u> believing.

Eloquent Expression

FIGURES OF SPEECH
Representative, not exhaustive.

Personification in "Hiawatha": whispering of the pine-trees, lapping of the waters, said the pine trees, said the water, dancing...creature, moon rise from the water, wildflowers...fade and perish

Simile in "Hiawatha": (none)

Lesson 10.4

SCANSION:

   | /∪| / ∪| / ∪| / ∪ |
Right a gainst the moon he threw her;

   | / ∪ |/ ∪| / ∪| / ∪ |
'T is her bod y that you see there."

| / ∪ | / ∪ |/ ∪ | / ∪ |
Saw the rain bow in the hea ven,

| / ∪ | / ∪ | / ∪ | / ∪ |
In the east ern sky, the rain bow,

| / ∪ | / ∪ | / ∪ | / ∪ |
Whis pered, "What is that, No ko mis?"

| / ∪ | / ∪ | / ∪ | / ∪ |
And the good No ko mis ans wered:

| / ∪ | / ∪ | / ∪ | / ∪ |
"'T is the heav'n of flow'rs you see there;

| / ∪ | / ∪ | / ∪ | / ∪ |
All the wild-flow'rs of the for est,

| / ∪ | / ∪ | / ∪ | / ∪ |
All the lil ies of the prai rie,

| / ∪ | / ∪ | / ∪ | / ∪ |
When on earth they fade and pe rish,

| / ∪ | / ∪ | / ∪ | / ∪ |
Blos som in that heav'n a bove us."

VERBALS: THE INFINITIVE

1. To see is to believe. 2. Flee from the wrath to come. He lived to die, and died to live.

WORD	PART OF SPEECH	DEFINE	CLASSIFY	PROPERTIES	FUNCTION
1. to see	verbal	*to see*	infinitive	--	noun, subject
1. to believe	verbal	*to believe*	infinitive	--	noun, PN *is*

WORD	PART OF SPEECH	DEFINE	CLASSIFY	PROPERTIES	FUNCTION
2. to come	verbal	*to come*	infinitive	--	adjectival, modifies *wrath*
3. to die	verbal	*to die*	infinitive	--	adverbial, modifies *lived*
3. to live	verbal	*to live*	infinitive	--	adverbial, modifies *died*

1. To see is to believe.

2. Flee (from the wrath) to come.

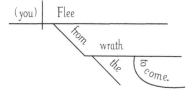

3. He lived to die, and died to live.

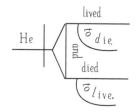

Eloquent Expression

LITERARY IMITATION

The Nile cut its way (between tall cliffs,) flecked (with passing shadows), and lifting clear outlines (against a bright blue sky.)

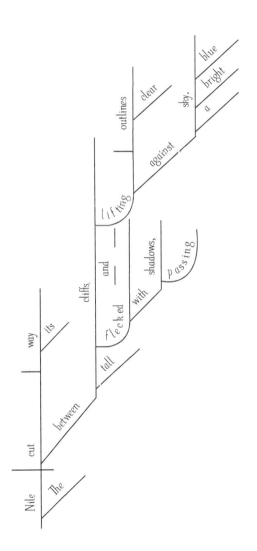

Lesson 10.5

Language Logic

SENTENCE DIAGRAMMING AND PARSING

(At the door) (on summer evenings) <u>Sat</u> the little <u>Hiawatha</u>; Heard
the whispering (of the pine-trees,) Heard the lapping (of the waters).

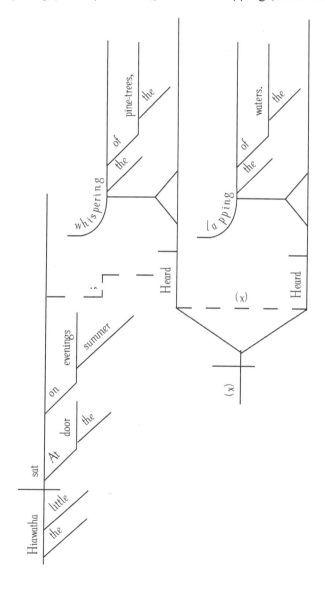

WORD	PART OF SPEECH	DEFINE	CLASSIFY	PROPERTIES	FUNCTION
At the door	prepo-sitional phrase	relates *door* to *sat*	--	--	adverbial, modifies *sat*
heard	verb	action	transitive	3rd singular past	main verb of a princi-pal clause
whispering	verbal	*to whis-per*	gerund	present	DO *heard*
of the pine-trees	prepo-sitional phrase	relates *trees* to *whisper-ing*	--	--	adjectival, modifies *whispering*
lapping	verbal	*to lap*	gerund	present	DO *heard*

Lesson 11

❧

THE BOSTON TEA PARTY

from AMERICAN HISTORY STORIES, PART II **by** Mara L. Pratt

[Prologue] This Boston tea-party was a very different sort of a party from the quiet little tea-parties to which your mammas like to go. There were no invitations sent out for this tea-party, and the people who attended it behaved in a very queer way, considering they were at a tea-party.

This was the way it came about. The English had put a tax, you will remember, upon nearly everything, tea included.

Now, when they found that the colonists were so furious about it, and seemed so determined to stand up for their rights, the English began to be afraid, and to think that perhaps they had gone a little too far.

So, wishing to soothe the angry colonists, they took off the tax on everything except the tea. "We will keep the tax on that," said the English, "just to let the colonists know that we have the power to tax them, and that they must obey; but we will not ask them to give us their money on the other things."

Foolish people, to suppose the colonists were going to be quieted in that way. It wasn't the money that they were made to pay that had angered them; they were willing to pay that; but it was the idea of their being taxed without representation!

"Does England suppose it is the few paltry dollars that we care for?" said they. "No; we will show her that, while we would be willing to pay thousands of dollars if we were treated fairly, we will not pay one cent when she treats us like slaves!"

[Action 1] Not many days had passed before word came that a great vessel, loaded with tea, was nearing the harbor.

[Action 2 – Place] A lively meeting was held in Faneuil Hall, and afterwards in the Old South Church; and the people all declared that the tea should never be allowed to be brought ashore.

[Action 3 – Time] At evening the vessel was seen slowly nearing the wharf. Everything was quiet, and you would never have imagined what was going to happen.

Slowly the ship comes in, nearer and nearer the little wharf. Now, with a heavy swash of water and a boom, she touches; out jump her sailors to fasten her ropes.

[Action 4 – Person] But hark! what noise is that? It is the Indian war-whoop. And see! down rush the Indians themselves, yelling and brandishing their tomahawks. In an instant they have boarded the vessel. Down into the hold they go, yelling and whooping at every step.

The terrified sailors stand back aghast. Out they come again, lugging with them their heavy chests of tea.

Still they yell and whoop; and over go the chests into the dark water below.

[Action 5 – Manner] And now, when every chest is gone, suddenly the Indians grow very quiet; they come off from the deck; and, orderly, take their stand upon the wharf; then do we see that they were not Indians at all. They were only men of Boston disguised.

[Author Comment] This then was the Boston tea-party, which took place in Boston Harbor on the evening of December 16, 1773. Three hundred and forty-two chests were thrown overboard.

[Action 6 – Place] On their way home the party passed the house at which Admiral Montague was spending the evening. The officer raised the window and cried out, "Well, boys, you've had a fine night for your Indian caper. But, mind, you've got to pay the fiddler yet." "Oh, never mind," replied one of the leaders, "never mind, squire! Just come out here, if you please, and we'll settle the bill in two minutes." The admiral thought it best to let the bill stand, and quickly shut the window.

[Epilogue] The Americans had taken one great step towards liberty, and the English had been taught a lesson of American grit. It would have been well for England had she been wise enough to heed it.

CR

Lesson 11.1

Prose & Poetry

LITERARY ELEMENTS

3 Observe the Invention and Arrangement

◆ **Lyrical Elements**

- Describes
- Senses
- Comparisons

◆ **Narrative Elements**

- **Setting** Boston, Massachusetts, December 16, 1773
- **Characters** Colonists, English, "Indians," sailors, Admiral Montague (notice he is the only particular person actually named)
- **Conflict** The English have imposed a tax on the colonists. The colonists are furious and want to show the English they will not be treated so.
- **Resolution** Colonists successfully destroy the tea cargo

4 Investigate the Context

◆ Identify the poem's **Literary Genre**

- **Genre by literary period** – 19th century American (children's)
- **Genre by poetic/narrative category** – non-fiction

Lesson 11.2

Language Logic

SENTENCE DIAGRAMMING AND PARSING

Wishing to soothe the angry colonists, they removed the tax (on everything) (except the tea.)

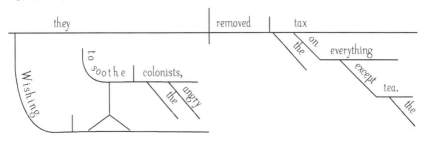

WORD	PART OF SPEECH	DEFINE	CLASSIFY	PROPERTIES	FUNCTION
Wishing	verbal	*to wish*	participle	present	adjectival – modifying *they*
to soothe	verbal	*to soothe*	infinitive	--	noun – DO *wishing*
colonists	noun	person	common	3rd plural common	Object of infinitive *to soothe*
except the tea	prepositional phrase	relates *tea* to *everything*	--	--	adjectival – modifies *everything*

Eloquent Expression

COPIA OF CONSTRUCTION: ADJECTIVE PLACEMENT

Answers will vary: 1. The colonists, furious, were determined to stand up for their rights. 2. Over go the chests into the water dark.

COPIA OF CONSTRUCTION: ADVERB PLACEMENT

Answers will vary: 3. The ship comes slowly in. The ship comes in slowly. The ship slowly comes in. 4. The admiral then quickly shut the window quickly. The admiral shut the window then, quickly.

Lesson 11.3

Prose & Poetry

NARRATIVE PLOT ANALYSIS

See suggested scene divisions in selection at beginning of this lesson. Remember that answers may vary.

Language Logic

SENTENCE DIAGRAMMING AND PARSING

A great vessel, loaded with tea, was nearing the harbor.

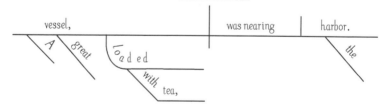

WORD	PART OF SPEECH	DEFINE	CLASSIFY	PROPERTIES	FUNCTION
A	adjective	modifies a noun	definitive – article	--	modifies *vessel*
loaded	verbal	*to load*	participle	perfect	adjectival modifying *vessel*
was nearing	verb	action	transitive	3rd singular past	main verb of sentence
harbor	noun	place	common	3rd singular neuter	DO *was nearing*

Eloquent Expression

COPIA OF CONSTRUCTION: PHRASE PLACEMENT – ADJECTIVE

Answers will vary: 1. Terrified, the sailors stand back. The sailors stand back, terrified. 2. Lugging their heavy chests of tea, they come out again.

COPIA OF CONSTRUCTION: PHRASE PLACEMENT – ADVERB

Answers will vary: 3. For this tea-party, no invitations were sent out. No invitations for this tea-party were sent out. 4. Slowly the vessel was seen nearing the wharf at evening. The vessel was seen at evening slowly nearing the wharf.

Lesson 11.4

Eloquent Expression

COPIA OF WORDS: VERB/VERBAL SWITCH

Answers will vary: 1. They wished to soothe the angry colonists by taking off the tax on everything except the tea. 2. The Indians themselves, rushing down, yell and brandish their tomahawks. Rushing down, the Indians themselves yell and brandish their tomahawks.

COPIA OF WORDS: GERUND/INFINITIVE SWITCH

Answers will vary: 3. The English began thinking that perhaps they had gone a little too far. 4. To be taxed without representation angered them!

Lesson 11.5

Eloquent Expression

LITERARY IMITATION

A little gypsy <u>wind</u> <u>came</u> (down the lane) to meet them, laden (with the spicy perfume) (of young dew wet ferns.)

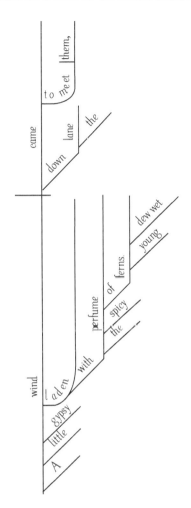

Lesson 12

THE BOSTON TEA PARTY
A First-Person Account by George Hewes

It was now evening, and I immediately dressed myself in the costume of an Indian, equipped with a small hatchet, which I and my associates denominated the tomahawk, with which, and a club, after having painted my face and hands with coal dust in the shop of a blacksmith, I repaired to Griffin's wharf, where the ships lay that contained the tea. When I first appeared in the street after being thus disguised, I fell in with many who were dressed, equipped and painted as I was, and who fell in with me and marched in order to the place of our destination.

When we arrived at the wharf, there were three of our number who assumed an authority to direct our operations, to which we readily submitted. They divided us into three parties, for the purpose of boarding the three ships which contained the tea at the same time. The name of him who commanded the division to which I was assigned was Leonard Pitt. The names of the other commanders I never knew.

We were immediately ordered by the respective commanders to board all the ships at the same time, which we promptly obeyed. The commander of the division to which I belonged, as soon as we were on board the ship appointed me boatswain, and ordered me to go to the captain and demand of him the keys to the hatches and a dozen candles. I made the demand accordingly, and the captain promptly replied, and delivered the articles; but requested me at the same time to do no damage to the ship or rigging.

We then were ordered by our commander to open the hatches and take out all the chests of tea and throw them overboard, and we immediately proceeded to execute his orders, first cutting and splitting the chests with our tomahawks, so as thoroughly to expose them to the effects of the water.

In about three hours from the time we went on board, we had thus broken and thrown overboard every tea chest to be found in the ship, while those in the other ships were disposing of the tea in the same way, at the same time. We were surrounded by British armed ships, but no attempt was made to resist us.

We then quietly retired to our several places of residence, without having any conversation with each other, or taking any measures to discover who were our associates; nor do I recollect of our having had the knowledge of the name of a single individual concerned in that affair, except that of Leonard Pitt, the commander of my division, whom I have mentioned. There appeared to be an understanding that each individual should volunteer his services, keep his own secret, and risk the consequence for himself. No disorder took place during that transaction, and it was observed at that time that the stillest night ensued that Boston had enjoyed for many months.

During the time we were throwing the tea overboard, there were several attempts made by some of the citizens of Boston and its vicinity to carry off small quantities of it for their family use. To effect that object, they would watch their opportunity to snatch up a handful from the deck, where it became plentifully scattered, and put it into their pockets.

One Captain O'Connor, whom I well knew, came on board for that purpose, and when he supposed he was not noticed, filled his pockets, and also the lining of his coat. But I had detected him and gave information to the captain of what he was doing. We were ordered to take him into custody, and just as he was stepping from the vessel, I seized him by the skirt of his coat, and in attempting to pull him back, I tore it off; but, springing forward, by a rapid effort he made his escape. He had, however, to run a gauntlet through the crowd upon the wharf nine each one, as he passed, giving him a kick or a stroke.

Another attempt was made to save a little tea from the ruins of the cargo by a tall, aged man who wore a large cocked hat and white wig, which was fashionable at that time. He had sleightly slipped a little into his pocket, but being detected, they seized him and, taking his hat and wig from his head, threw them, together with the tea, of which they had emptied his pockets, into the water. In consideration of his advanced age, he was permitted to escape, with now and then a slight kick.

The next morning, after we had cleared the ships of the tea, it was discovered that very considerable quantities of it were floating upon the surface of the water; and to prevent the possibility of any of its being saved for use, a number of small boats were manned by sailors and citizens, who rowed them into those parts of the harbor wherever the tea was visible, and by beating it with oars and paddles so thoroughly drenched it as to render its entire destruction inevitable.

Lesson 12.1

Prose & Poetry

LITERARY ELEMENTS

3 **Observe the Invention and Arrangement**
- ◆ **Narrative Elements** (see Lesson 11.1 also)
  - ■ **Characters** George Hewes, men dressed in Indian costume, Leonard Pitt, British captain, citizens of Boston, Captain O'Connor

4 **Investigate the Context**
- ◆ Identify the poem's **Literary Genre**
  - ■ **Genre by literary period** – 18th century American
  - ■ **Genre by poetic/narrative category** – non-fiction

Lesson 12.2

Language Logic

SENTENCE DIAGRAMMING AND PARSING

Out they come again, lugging (with them) their heavy chests (of tea.)

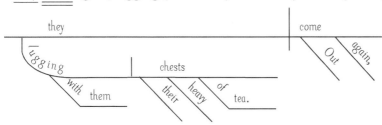

WORD	PART OF SPEECH	DEFINE	CLASSIFY	PROPERTIES	FUNCTION
Out	adverb	modifies a verb	--	--	modifies *come*
lugging	verbal	*to lug*	participle	present	adjectival, modifies *they*
their	pronoun	*Indians*	possessive	3rd plural masculine	modifies *chests;* shows possession
heavy	adjective	modifies a noun	descriptive	--	modifies *chests*
of tea	prepositional phrase	relates tea to *chests*	--	--	adjectival, modifies *chests*

Lesson 12.3

Language Logic

SENTENCE DIAGRAMMING AND PARSING

They <u>were</u> only men of Boston disguised.

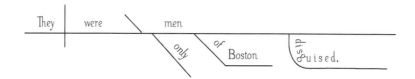

WORD	PART OF SPEECH	DEFINE	CLASSIFY	PROPERTIES	FUNCTION
They	pronoun	*Indians*	personal	3rd plural masculine	subject of principal clause
were	verb	state/being	linking	3rd plural past	main verb of principal clause
only	adjective	modifies a noun	definitve	--	modifies *men*
men	noun	person	common	3rd plural masculine	predicate nominative
of Boston	prepositional phrase	relates *Boston* to *men*	--	--	modifies *men*
disguised	verbal	*to disguise*	participle	perfect	modifies *men*

Lesson 13

❦

A Visit From St. Nicholas

'Twas the night before Christmas, when all through the house
Not a creature was stirring, not even a mouse;
The stockings were hung by the chimney with care,
In hopes that St. Nicholas soon would be there;
The children were nestled all snug in their beds;
While visions of sugar-plums danced in their heads;
And mamma in her 'kerchief, and I in my cap,
Had just settled our brains for a long winter's nap,
When out on the lawn there arose such a clatter,
I sprang from my bed to see what was the matter.
Away to the window I flew like a flash,
Tore open the shutters and threw up the sash.
The moon on the breast of the new-fallen snow,
Gave a lustre of midday to objects below,
When what to my wondering eyes did appear,
But a miniature sleigh and eight tiny rein-deer,
With a little old driver so lively and quick,
I knew in a moment he must be St. Nick.
More rapid than eagles his coursers they came,
And he whistled, and shouted, and called them by name:
"Now, Dasher! now, Dancer! now Prancer and Vixen!
On, Comet! on, Cupid! on, Donder and Blixen!
To the top of the porch! to the top of the wall!
Now dash away! dash away! dash away all!"
As leaves that before the wild hurricane fly,
When they meet with an obstacle, mount to the sky;
So up to the housetop the coursers they flew
With the sleigh full of toys, and St. Nicholas too—
And then, in a twinkling, I heard on the roof
The prancing and pawing of each little hoof.
As I drew in my head, and was turning around,

Down the chimney St. Nicholas came with a bound.
He was dressed all in fur, from his head to his foot,
And his clothes were all tarnished with ashes and soot;
A bundle of toys he had flung on his back,
And he looked like a peddler just opening his pack.
His eyes—how they twinkled! his dimples, how merry!
His cheeks were like roses, his nose like a cherry!
His droll little mouth was drawn up like a bow,
And the beard on his chin was as white as the snow;
The stump of a pipe he held tight in his teeth,
And the smoke, it encircled his head like a wreath;
He had a broad face and a little round belly
That shook when he laughed, like a bowl full of jelly.
He was chubby and plump, a right jolly old elf,
And I laughed when I saw him, in spite of myself;
A wink of his eye and a twist of his head
Soon gave me to know I had nothing to dread;
He spoke not a word, but went straight to his work,
And filled all the stockings; then turned with a jerk,
And laying his finger aside of his nose,
And giving a nod, up the chimney he rose;
He sprang to his sleigh, to his team gave a whistle,
And away they all flew like the down of a thistle.
But I heard him exclaim, ere he drove out of sight—
"Happy Christmas to all, and to all a good night!"

—CLEMENT CLARKE MOORE

Lesson 13.1

Prose & Poetry

LITERARY ELEMENTS

3 Observe the Invention and Arrangement
◆ **Lyrical Elements**
- He describes St. Nicholas in detail; also describes the Action outside his window, the reindeer, and the arrival of the sleigh.
- He makes you "see" St. Nicholas, "hear" the clatter.
- He compares dreams to sugarplums, St. Nicholas to a peddler with a pack, and his personal features to many everyday things (see Lesson 10.3 Eloquent Expression).

◆ **Narrative Elements**
- **Setting** the night before Christmas
- **Characters** I (presumably the father of the family), mama, children, St. Nick
- **Conflict** What was going to happen in this fantastical situation?
- **Resolution** St. Nick arrived in his sleigh, came down the chimney, filled the stockings, went back up the chimney, and left.

4 Investigate the Context
◆ Identify the poem's **Literary Genre**
- **Genre by literary period** – 19th century American
- **Genre by poetic/narrative category** – lyrical

Language Logic

SENTENCE DIAGRAMMING AND PARSING

And then, (in a twinkling,) I heard (on the roof)

The prancing and pawing (of each little hoof.)

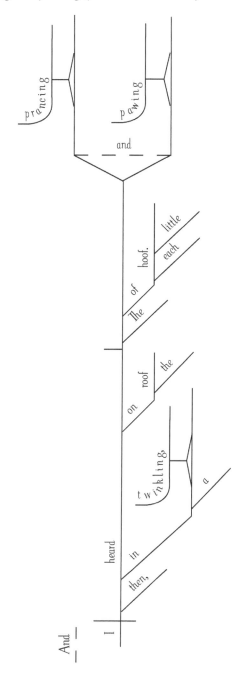

WORD	PART OF SPEECH	DEFINE	CLASSIFY	PROPERTIES	FUNCTION
twinkling	verbal	*to twinkle*	gerund	present	OP *in*
heard	verb	shows action	transitive	1st singular past	main verb
on the roof	prepo- sitional phrase	relates *roof* to *heard*	--	--	adverbial – modify- ing *heard*
prancing	verbal	*to prance*	gerund	present	DO *heard*

Lesson 13.2

Prose & Poetry

SCANSION AND ANALYSIS

Rhyme Scheme: AABBCCDD . . .

Stanza Name: n/a, although it could be classified as couplet because of the rhyme scheme.

Poetic Meter: anapestic tetrameter

SCANSION:

```
|  ᴗ  ᴗ  / |ᴗ ᴗ  /  ᴗ   ᴗ  /|  ᴗ    ᴗ  /  |
```
'Twas the night be fore Christ mas, when all through the house

```
| ᴗ ᴗ  /|ᴗ  ᴗ  /|ᴗ   ᴗ /|ᴗ ᴗ   / |
```
Not a crea ture was stir ring, not e ven a mouse;

```
| ᴗ  / | ᴗ   ᴗ   / |ᴗ ᴗ   /|ᴗ  ᴗ  / |
```
The stock ings were hung by the chim ney with care,

```
| ᴗ  / |  ᴗ  ᴗ  / |ᴗᴗ  /  |  ᴗ   ᴗ  / |
```
In hopes that St. Nich o las soon would be there;

| ∪ / |∪ ∪ /|∪ ∪ / |∪ ∪   / |
The child ren were nes tled all snug in their beds;

| ∪ /|∪ ∪ /|∪ ∪   / |∪∪   / |
While vi sions of sug ar-plums danced in their heads;

| ∪ ∪ /|∪∪ /| ∪   ∪/|∪∪ /|
And mam ma in her 'ker chief, and I in my cap,

| ∪ ∪ /|∪ ∪ / |∪∪ /|∪ ∪   /|
Had just set tled our brains for a long win ter's nap,

| ∪   /|∪∪   /| ∪ ∪ / |∪ ∪ / ∪|
When out on the lawn there a rose such a clat ter,

|∪ / | ∪ ∪ /|∪∪ / | ∪ ∪ / ∪|
I sprang from my bed to see what was the mat ter.

|∪ /|∪ ∪ / | ∪ ∪ / |∪∪   /|
A way to the win dow I flew like a flash,

| ∪ /|∪ ∪ / |∪ ∪ / | ∪ ∪   / |
Tore o pen the shut ters and threw up the sash.

| ∪   /|∪ ∪   / |∪∪   /| ∪ ∪ / |
The moon on the breast of the new-fal len snow,

| ∪ ∪/|∪∪ / |∪ ∪/| ∪ ∪ /|
Gave a lus tre of mid day to ob jects be low,

| ∪ / |∪ ∪   /|∪ ∪ / |∪∪ /|
When what to my won der ing eyes did ap pear,

|∪∪ /|∪ ∪ / | ∪ ∪ / |∪∪   /|
But a min ia ture sleigh and eight ti ny rein-deer,

| ∪ ∪/|∪ ∪ /|∪∪ / |∪ ∪   / |
With a lit tle old driv er so live ly and quick,

|∪ / |∪∪ /| ∪ ∪   / |∪∪   / |
I knew in a mo ment he must be St. Nick.

Other Anapestic Poems: "The Destruction of Sennacherib" is anapestic tetrameter.

Language Logic

PARSING THE CONJUNCTION – HARVEY'S EXERCISE 146

2. He'd sooner die than ask you, or any man, for a shilling.
4. Neither military nor civil pomp was wanting. 7. I alone was solitary and idle. 9. There was no reply, for a slight fear was upon every man. 13. Not a having and resting, but a growing and becoming, is the true character of perfection as culture conceives it.

WORD	PART OF SPEECH	DEFINE	CLASSIFY	PROPERTIES	FUNCTION
2. than	conjunc-tion	con-nects two clauses	subordi-nate	--	connects subordi-nate clause to princi-pal clause
2. or	conjunc-tion	con-nects two words	coordinate	--	connects *you* and *man*
4. Neither	conjunc-tion	con-nects two words	coordi-nate, cor-relative	--	connects *military* and *civil*
4. nor	conjunc-tion	con-nects two words	coordi-nate, cor-relative	--	connects *military* and *civil*
7. and	conjunc-tion	con-nects two words	coordinate	--	connects *solitary* and *idle*
9. for	conjunc-tion	con-nects two clauses	coordinate	--	connects two princi pal clauses
13. and	conjunc-tion	con-nects two words	coordinate	--	connects *having* and *resting*
13. but	conjunc-tion	con-nects two phrases	coordinate	--	connects compound subjects

WORD	PART OF SPEECH	DEFINE	CLASSIFY	PROPERTIES	FUNCTION
13. and	conjunc-tion	con-nects two words	coordinate	--	connects *grow-ing* and *becoming*
13. as	conjunc-tion	con-nects two clauses	subordi-nate	--	connects subordi-nate clause to princi-pal clause

---

Lesson 13.3

Prose & Poetry

SCANSION:

| ∪ / |∪ ∪ / |∪ ∪ / | ∪ ∪ / |
More rap id than ea gles his cours ers they came,

| ∪ ∪ / | ∪ ∪ / |∪ ∪ / | ∪ ∪ / |
And he whis tled, and shout ed, and called them by name:

| ∪ / |∪ ∪ / |∪ ∪ / |∪∪ / ∪|
"Now, Dash er! now, Danc er! now Pranc er and Vix en!

| ∪ / |∪ ∪ / |∪ ∪ / |∪ ∪ / ∪|
On, Com et! on, Cu pid! on, Don der and Blix en!

| ∪ ∪ / |∪∪ / | ∪∪ / |∪∪ / |
To the top of the porch! to the top of the wall!

| ∪ / |∪∪ / |∪∪ / |∪∪ / |
Now dash a way! dash a way! dash a way all!"

|∪ / | ∪ ∪ / |∪ ∪ / |∪∪ / |
As leaves that be fore the wild hur ri cane fly,

| ∪   ∪   / | ∪   ∪ /| ∪   ∪   / | ∪∪   / |

When they meet with an ob sta cle, mount to the sky;

| ∪ /| ∪∪ / | ∪ ∪ / | ∪   ∪ / |

So up to the house top the cours ers they flew

| ∪   ∪   / | ∪ ∪ /| ∪ ∪ / | ∪∪ / |

With the sleigh full of toys, and St. Nich o las too—

| ∪ / | ∪∪ / | ∪∪ / | ∪ ∪ / |

And then, in a twink ling, I heard on the roof

| ∪   / | ∪ ∪ /| ∪ ∪ / | ∪∪ / |

The pranc ing and paw ing of each lit tle hoof.

| ∪∪ / | ∪∪ / | ∪   ∪ / | ∪ ∪ /|

As I drew in my head, and was turn ing a round,

| ∪ ∪ / | ∪∪ / | ∪∪ / | ∪ ∪ / |

Down the chim ney St. Nich o las came with a bound.

| ∪   ∪ / | ∪∪ /| ∪   ∪ / | ∪ ∪ /|

He was dressed all in fur, from his head to his foot,

| ∪   ∪ / | ∪   ∪ /| ∪   ∪ / | ∪ ∪ / |

And his clothes were all tar nished with ash es and soot;

| ∪ / | ∪ ∪ / | ∪∪ / | ∪ ∪ / |

A bun dle of toys he had flung on his back,

| ∪   ∪ / | ∪ ∪ /| ∪ ∪ /| ∪   ∪ / |

And he looked like a ped dler just o pening his pack.

Language Logic

SENTENCE DIAGRAMMING

1. [(At length,) the sun departed, setting (in a sea) (of gold.)] – Principal
Clause

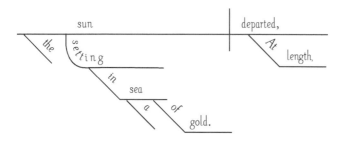

2. [The heavens declare the glory of God,] and [the firmament shows His
handiwork.] – Both are Principal Clauses

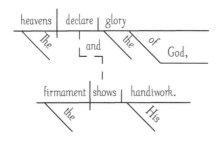

3. He [that refuseth instruction] despiseth his own soul.] – *He despiseth
his own soul* is a principal clause; *that refuseth instruction* is a subordinate clause

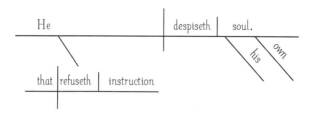

4. [I am the bread (of life)]: [he [that cometh (to me)] shall never hunger.]
– *I am the bread of life* is a principal clause; *he shall never hunger* is a
principal clause; *that cometh to me* is a subordinate clause

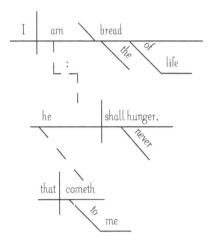

Eloquent Expression

FIGURES OF SPEECH IDENTIFICATION
Representative, not exhaustive.

Personification in "A Visit From St. Nicholas": visions danced,
wondering eyes, leaves that...fly, prancing and pawing of each little hoof

Simile in "A Visit From St. Nicholas": he flew like a flash, more
rapid than eagles, as leaves...before the wild hurricane fly, he looked like
a peddler...opening his sack, his cheeks were like roses, his nose like a
cherry, mouth was drawn up like a bow, beard...as white as the snow,
smoke...like a wreath, belly...shook like a bowl full of jelly, flew like the
down of a thistle.

Lesson 13.4

Prose & Poetry

SCANSION:

| ∪ / |∪∪ / | ∪ ∪ / |∪∪ / |
The stump of a pipe he held tight in his teeth,

| ∪ ∪ / |∪∪ / | ∪ ∪ / |∪∪ / |
And the smoke, it en cir cled his head like a wreath;

| ∪ / |∪ ∪ / |∪∪ / |∪ ∪ / ∪|
He had a broad face and a lit tle round bel ly

| ∪ / | ∪ ∪ / |∪∪ / | ∪ ∪ / ∪|
That shook when he laughed, like a bowl full of jel ly.

| ∪ ∪ / |∪ ∪ / |∪∪ / |∪ ∪ / |
He was chub by and plump, a right jol ly old elf,

| ∪ ∪ / | ∪ ∪ / | ∪ ∪ / |∪∪ / |
And I laughed when I saw him, in spite of my self;

|∪ / |∪∪ / |∪∪ / |∪∪ / |
A wink of his eye and a twist of his head

| ∪ / |∪ ∪ / |∪ ∪ / |∪ ∪ / |
Soon gave me to know I had noth ing to dread;

|∪ / |∪ ∪ / |∪ ∪ / |∪∪ / |
He spoke not a word, but went straight to his work,

| ∪ / |∪∪ / |∪ ∪ / | ∪ ∪ / |
And filled all the stock ings; then turned with a jerk,

| ∪ / |∪ ∪ / |∪∪ / |∪ ∪ / |
And lay ing his fin ger a side of his nose,

| ∪ ∕| ∪∪ ∕|∪∪ ∕| ∪ ∪ ∕ |

And giv ing a nod, up the chim ney he rose;

|∪ ∕ |∪∪ ∕ | ∪∪ ∕|∪ ∪ ∕ ∪|

He sprang to his sleigh, to his team gave a whis tle,

|∪ ∪ ∕|∪ ∪ ∕ |∪ ∪ ∕|∪∪ ∕ ∪|

And a way they all flew like the down of a this tle.

|∪ ∪ ∕ |∪ ∪ ∕ | ∪∪ ∕ |∪∪ ∕ |

But I heard him ex claim, ere he drove out of sight—

| ∪ ∪ ∕ | ∪ ∪ ∕| ∪∪ ∕|∪∪ ∕ |

"Hap py Christ mas to all, and to all a good night!"

Language Logic

SENTENCE CLASS BY FORM IDENTIFICATION
1. Simple, 2. Compound, 3. Complex, 4. Compound-Complex

Eloquent Expression

LITERARY IMITATION
[Heaven above was blue,] [and earth beneath was green]; [the river glis-
tened (like a path) (of diamonds) (in the sun)];] [the birds poured forth
their songs (from the shady trees);] [the lark soared high (above the waving corn)]; and [the deep buzz (of insects) filled the air.]

– compound sentence

Figures of Description: chronographia, topographia

Figures of Speech: parallelism (Heaven above was blue, and earth beneath was green), simile (like a path of diamonds), personification (waving corn, deep buzz filled)

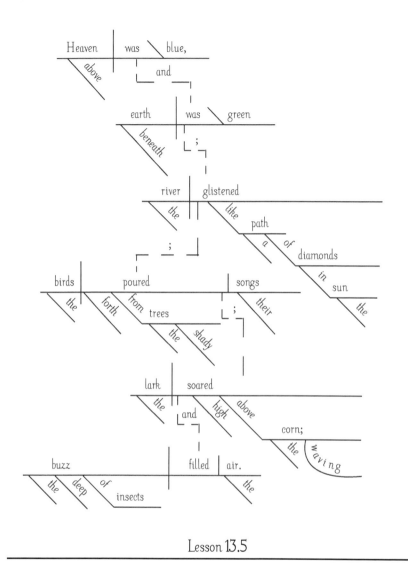

Lesson 13.5

LANGUAGE LOGIC

SENTENCE DIAGRAMMING AND PARSING

And [mamma (in her 'kerchief), and I (in my cap,)
Had just settled our brains (for a long winter nap.)]   – *simple sentence*

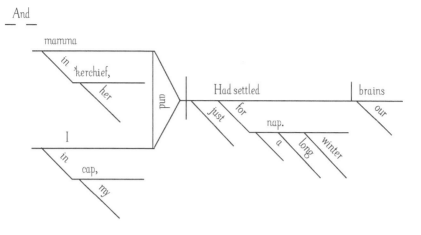

WORD	PART OF SPEECH	DEFINE	CLASSIFY	PROPERTIES	FUNCTION
mamma	noun	person	proper*	3rd singular feminine	subject
in my cap	prepositional phrase	relates *cap* to *I*	--	--	adjectival – modifiying *I*
just	adverb	modifies a verb	--	--	modifies *had settled*
long	adjective	modifies a noun	descriptive	--	modifies *nap*
winter	adjective	modifies a noun	descriptive	--	modifies *nap*

Mamma here is a proper noun, since it does refer to a particular person, even though it is not capitalized. Chalk it up to poetic license!

❧

THE CHARGE OF THE LIGHT BRIGADE

I.

Half a league, half a league,
 Half a league onward,
All in the valley of Death
  Rode the six hundred.
"Forward, the Light Brigade!
"Charge for the guns!" he said:
Into the valley of Death
  Rode the six hundred.

II.

"Forward, the Light Brigade!"
Was there a man dismay'd?
Not tho' the soldier knew
  Someone had blunder'd:
  Theirs not to make reply,
  Theirs not to reason why,
  Theirs but to do and die:
  Into the valley of Death
  Rode the six hundred.

III.

Cannon to right of them,
Cannon to left of them,
Cannon in front of them
  Volley'd and thunder'd;
Into the jaws of Death,
Into the mouth of Hell
  Rode the six hundred.

IV.

Flash'd all their sabres bare,
Flash'd as they turn'd in air,
Sabring the gunners there,
Charging an army, while
  All the world wonder'd:
Plunged in the battery-smoke
Right thro' the line they broke;
Cossack and Russian
Reel'd from the sabre stroke
  Shatter'd and sunder'd.
Then they rode back, but not
  Not the six hundred.

V.

Cannon to right of them,
Cannon to left of them,
Cannon behind them
  Volley'd and thunder'd;
Storm'd at with shot and shell,
While horse and hero fell,
They that had fought so well
Came thro' the jaws of Death
Back from the mouth of Hell,
All that was left of them,
  Left of six hundred.

VI.

When can their glory fade?
O the wild charge they made!

All the world wondered.
Honor the charge they made,
Honor the Light Brigade,
  Noble six hundred.

— ALFRED, LORD TENNYSON

ᬓᬭ

Lesson 14.1

Prose & Poetry

LITERARY ELEMENTS

3 Observe the Invention and Arrangement

◆ Lyrical Elements

- He describes battle.

- He makes you "see" and "hear" the confusion and noise of battle.

- He compares the battlefield to Death and Hell.

◆ Narrative Elements

- **Setting** Battle of Balaclava, October 25, 1854, in Russia during the Crimean War

- **Characters** The Light Brigade soldiers

- **Conflict** Due to a misunderstood dispatch, the Light Brigade was ordered to make a charge which they knew to be senseless.

- **Resolution** They chose to obey rather than question the order of a superior. Most were slaughtered, but they are remembered with honor.

4 **Investigate the Context**
- ◆ Identify the poem's **Literary Genre**
  - ■ **Genre by literary period** – 19th century English (Victorian)
  - ■ **Genre by poetic/narrative category** – narrative

Language Logic

SENTENCE DIAGRAMMING AND PARSING

[Plunged (in the battery-smoke)
Right (thro' the line) they broke.]   – *simple sentence*

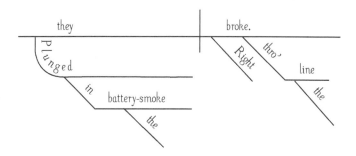

WORD	PART OF SPEECH	DEFINE	CLASSIFY	PROPERTIES	FUNCTION
Plunged	verbal	to plunge	participle	perfect	modifies *they*
right	adverb	modifies verb	--	--	modifies *broke*
thro' the line	prepo- sitional phrase	relates *line to broke*	--	--	adverbial – modifies *broke*
the	adjective	definitive – article	--	--	modifies *line*
they	pronoun	*soldiers of the Light Brigade*	personal	3rd plural masculine	subject

WORD	PART OF SPEECH	DEFINE	CLASSIFY	PROPERTIES	FUNCTION
broke	verb	action	intransitive	3rd plural past	main verb

Lesson 14.2

Prose & Poetry

SCANSION AND ANALYSIS

Rhyme Scheme: ABCBDDCB, AABCDDDEF, AAABCCDCB,

AAABCDDEDCFC, AAABCCCDCAB, AABAAB

Stanza Name: Stanza 1 – octave, Stanzas 2 & 3 have 9 lines each,

Stanza 4 has 12 lines, Stanza 5 has 11 lines, and Stanza 6 is a hexastitch.

Nota Bene: *The erratic and somewhat chaotic rhyme scheme and stanza arrangement echoes the chaos of battle. The rhyme scheme does settle into a more regular scheme in the final stanza; perhaps because it deals with "the way things should be" – the nobility of the soldiers and their deed will be remembered and honored.*

Poetic Meter: primarily dactylic dimeter, with a few lines of trimeter

SCANSION:

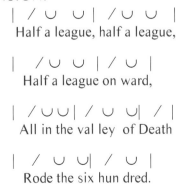

| / ∪ ∪| / ∪ ∪|
"For ward, the Light Brig ade!

| / ∪ ∪| / ∪ ∪|
"Charge for the guns!" he said:

| /∪ ∪| / ∪ ∪| / |
In to the val ley of Death

| / ∪ ∪| / ∪ |
Rode the six hun dred.

| / ∪ ∪| / ∪ ∪ |
"For ward, the Light Brig ade!"

| / ∪ ∪| / ∪ ∪ |
Was there a man dis may'd?

| / ∪ ∪| / ∪ ∪ |
Not tho' the sol dier knew

| / ∪ ∪| / ∪ |
Some one had blun der'd:

| / ∪ ∪| / ∪ ∪|
Theirs not to make re ply,

| / ∪ ∪| / ∪ ∪ |
Theirs not to reas on why,

| / ∪ ∪| / ∪ ∪|
Theirs but to do and die:

| /∪ ∪| / ∪ ∪| / |
In to the val ley of Death

| / ∪ ∪| / ∪ |
Rode the six hun dred.

Other Dactylic Poems: "The Reading Mother" is dactylic tetrameter.

Language Logic

RELATIVE PRONOUNS – HARVEY'S EXERCISE 74.

1. Those who sow will reap. 2. He that hateth, dissembleth with his lips. 5. The house which you admire so much, belongs to the man whom we see yonder. 10. A kind boy avoids doing whatever injures others.

WORD	PART OF SPEECH	DEFINE	CLASSIFY	PROPERTIES	FUNCTION
1. who	pronoun	sowers	relative	3rd plural common	subject of subordinate clause
2. that	pronoun	hater	relative	3rd singular masculine	subject of subordinate clause
5. which	pronoun	*house*	relative	3rd singular neuter	DO *admire*
5. whom	pronoun	*man*	relative	3rd singular masculine	DO *see*
10. whatever	pronoun	injurious things	relative	3rd singular neuter	subject of subordinate clause

SENTENCE DIAGRAMMING

1. [I had a mother [who read (to me.)]]   – *complex sentence*

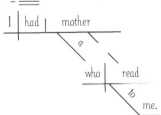

2. [How frugal is the chariot [that bears the human soul.]]

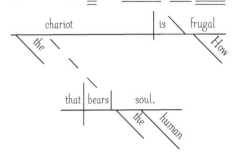

Lesson 14.3

Prose & Poetry

SCANSION:

```
| / ᴗ ᴗ| / ᴗ ᴗ |
```
Can non to right of them,

```
|  / ᴗ ᴗ|/ ᴗ  ᴗ |
```
Can non to left of them,

```
| / ᴗ ᴗ| / ᴗ  ᴗ|
```
Can non in front of them

```
|  / ᴗ  ᴗ| /  ᴗ |
```
Vol ley'd and thun der'd;

```
|   /  ᴗ ᴗ| /  ᴗ  ᴗ|
```
Storm'd at with shot and shell,

```
| / ᴗ  ᴗ | /  ᴗ ᴗ|
```
Bold ly they rode and well,

```
| /ᴗ ᴗ| / ᴗ  ᴗ |
```
In to the jaws of Death,

```
| /ᴗ  ᴗ| /  ᴗ ᴗ|
```
In to the mouth of Hell

```
|  / ᴗ  ᴗ| / ᴗ |
```
Rode the six hun dred.

| /   ∪ ∪ | / ∪   ∪ |
Flash'd all their sa bres bare,

| /   ∪ ∪ | /   ∪ ∪|
Flash'd as they turn'd in air,

| / ∪   ∪| /   ∪   ∪ |
Sa bring the gun ners there,

| /   ∪ ∪| / ∪   ∪|
Charg ing an ar my, while

| / ∪   ∪ | /   ∪ |
All the world won der'd:

| /   ∪ ∪| / ∪   ∪ |
Plunged in the bat tery-smoke

| /   ∪   ∪| / ∪   ∪ |
Right thro' the line they broke;

| / ∪   ∪| /   ∪ |
Cos sack and Rus sian

| /   ∪   ∪|/ ∪   ∪ |
Reel'd from the sa bre stroke

| / ∪   ∪| /   ∪ |
Shat ter'd and sun der'd.

| /   ∪   ∪| /   ∪ ∪|
Then they rode back, but not

| / ∪ ∪| / ∪ |
Not the six hun dred.

Language Logic

SENTENCE DIAGRAMMING

1. [[As he lay thinking,] he saw a spider (over his head.)]

– complex sentence

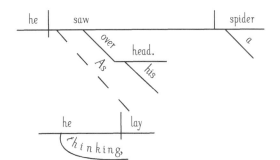

2. [(At evening) [when the lamp is lit,] (around the fire) my parents sit.]

– complex sentence

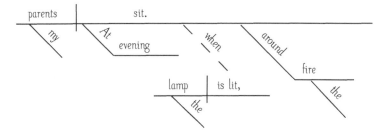

Eloquent Expression

COMPARISONS IN EXAMPLE METAPHORS

Man is compared to an island; the world is compared to a stage; time

compared to a sandglass; oak compared to a bulwark; praise of man

compared to a vapour.

FIGURES OF SPEECH – METAPHOR

Representative, not exhaustive.

Metaphor in "Charge of the Light Brigade": valley of Death, cannons

volley'd and thunder'd, jaws of Death, mouth of Hell

Metaphor in other poems: "The Farmer and His Sons": labor = treasure; "A Book": book = chariot; "Hiawatha": heaven of flowers

Simile and Personification in "Charge of the Light Brigade": none

---

Lesson 14.4

SCANSION:

| / ∪ ∪| / ∪ ∪ |
Can non to right of them,

| / ∪ ∪| / ∪ ∪ |
Can non to left of them,

| / ∪ ∪| / ∪ ∪ |
Can non in front of them

| / ∪ ∪| / ∪ |
Vol ley'd and thun der'd;

| / ∪ ∪| / ∪ ∪ |
Storm'd at with shot and shell,

| / ∪ ∪| / ∪ ∪ |
While horse and he ro fell,

| / ∪ ∪| / ∪ ∪ |
They that had fought so well

| / ∪ ∪| / ∪ ∪ |
Came thro' the jaws of Death

| / ∪ ∪| / ∪ ∪ |
Back from the mouth of Hell,

| / ∪ ∪| / ∪ ∪ |
All that was left of them,

| / ∪ ∪| / ∪ |
Left of six hun dred.

| / ∪ ∪ | / ∪ ∪ |
When can their glo ry fade?

| / ∪ ∪ | / ∪ ∪ |
O the wild charge they made!

| / ∪ ∪ | / ∪ |
All the world wond ered.

| / ∪ ∪| / ∪ ∪ |
Hon or the charge they made,

| / ∪ ∪| / ∪ ∪ |
Hon or the Light Brig ade,

| / ∪ ∪| / ∪ |
No ble six hun dred.

SENTENCE DIAGRAMMING

1. [My sons, heed [what I say (to you.)]]   – *complex sentence*

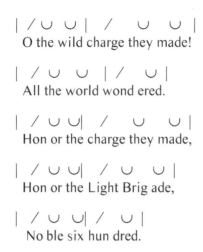

2. [[Where they would find the treasure] was not clear.]
                                              – *complex sentence*

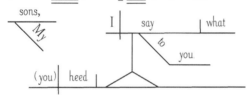

3. [Their wealth depended (upon [how hard they worked.)]]
                                              – *complex sentence*

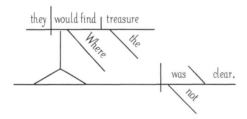

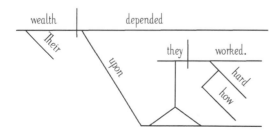

Eloquent Expression

LITERARY IMITATION

It came clear and cold, (with a touch (in the air) (like frost), and a
northerly wind) [that blew the clouds away and made the stars bright.]

– complex sentence

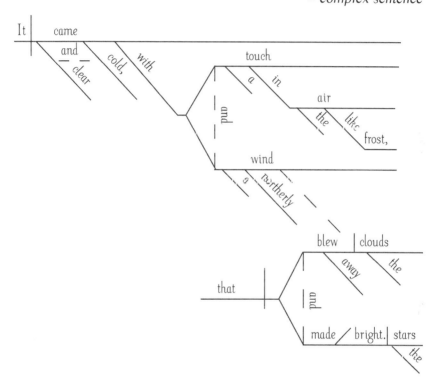

Figures of speech: simile – like frost; personification – wind blew and
made

Figures of description: astrothesia (vivid description of the night sky)
and anemographia (vivid description of the wind)

Lesson 14.5

Language Logic

SENTENCE DIAGRAMMING AND PARSING

[While horse and hero fell,]
[[They [that had fought so well]
Came (thro' the jaws) (of Death)
Back (from the mouth) (of Hell.]   *– complex sentence*

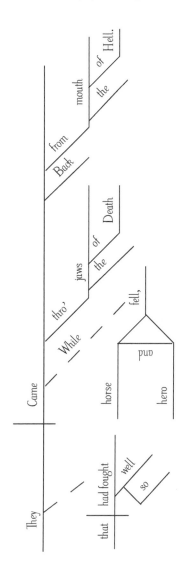

WORD	PART OF SPEECH	DEFINE	CLASSIFY	PROPERTIES	FUNCTION
While	conjunc-tion	connects clauses	subordi-nate	--	connects principal and sub-ordinate clauses
that	pronoun	*They (the Light Brigade)*	relative	3rd plural masculine	subject of subordi-nate clause
Back	adverb	modifies verb	--	--	modifies *came*
of Hell	prepo-sitional phrase	relates *Hell* to *mouth*	--	--	adjectival – modifies *mouth*

Lesson 15

☙

The Father of English Song

from English Literature for Boys and Girls by Henrietta Marshall

[Prologue] The Britons were Christian, for they had learned the story of Christ from the Romans. But when the Saxons conquered the land they robbed and ruined the churches, the Christian priests were slain or driven forth, and once more the land became heathen.

[Summary] Then, after many years had passed, the story of Christ was again brought to England. This time it came from Ireland. It was brought from there by St. Columba, who built a church and founded a monastery on the island of Iona. And from there his eager, wandering priests carried the story far and wide, northward to the fortress of the Pictish kings, and southward to the wild Saxons who dwelt amid the hills and uplands of Northumbria.

To this story of love and gentleness the wild heathen listened in wonder. To help the weak, to love and forgive their enemies, was something unthought of by these fierce sea-rovers. Yet they listened and believed. Once again churches were built, priests came to live among the people, and the sound of Christian prayer and praise rose night and morning from castle and from hut.

For thirty years and more St. Columba, the passionate and tender, taught and labored. Many monasteries were founded which became, as it were, the lighthouses of learning and religion. There the monks and priests lived, and from them as centers they traveled out in all directions teaching the heathen. And when at last St. Columba closed his tired eyes and folded his weary hands, there were many more to carry on his work.

Then, also, from Rome, as once before, the story of Christ was brought. In 597, the year in which St. Columba died, St. Augustine landed with his forty followers. They, too, in time reached Northumbria; so, side by side, Roman and Celt spoke the message of peace on earth, goodwill toward men.

The wild Saxon listened to this message, it is true. He took Christianity for his religion, but it was rather as if he had put on an outer dress. His new religion made little difference to his life. He still loved fighting and war, and his songs were still all of war. He worshiped Christ as he had worshiped Woden, and looked upon Him as a hero, only a little more powerful than the heroes of whom the minstrels sang. It was difficult to teach the Saxons the Bible lessons which we know so well, for in those far-off days there were no Bibles. There were indeed few books of any kind, and these few belonged to the monks and priests. They were in Latin, and in some of them parts of the Bible had been translated into Latin. But hardly any of the men and women of England could read or understand these books. Indeed, few people could read at all, for it was still the listening time. They learned the history of their country from the songs of the minstrels, and it was in this way, too, that they came to learn the Bible stories, for these stories were made into poetry. And it was among the rugged hills of Northumbria, by the rocky shore where the sounding waves beat and beat all day long, that the first Christian songs in English were sung. For here it was that Caedmon, the "Father of English Song," lived and died.

At Whitby there was a monastery ruled over by the Abbess Hilda. This was a post of great importance, for, as you know, the monasteries were the schools and libraries of the country, and they were the inns too, so all the true life of the land ebbed and flowed through the monasteries. Here priest and soldier, student and minstrel, prince and beggar came and went. Here in the great hall, when work was done and the evening meal over, were gathered all the monks and their guests. Here, too, would gather the simple folk of the countryside, the fishermen and farmers, the lay brothers and helpers who shared the work of the monastery. When the meal was done the minstrels sang, while proud and humble alike listened eagerly. Or perhaps "it was agreed for the sake of mirth that all present should sing in their turn."[1]

---

1   The author uses quotation marks from this point on to show where she has taken the words directly from the original author (Bede, translated in English). Note that within this quoted text, single quotation marks indicate the actual words of the characters. Note also that when a direct quotation (either of the author or a character) spans multiple paragraphs, quotation marks are only placed at the beginning of each paragraph. The lack of quotation marks at the end of the line indicate that the dialogue continues.

But when, at the monastery of Whitby, it was agreed that all should sing in turn, there was one among the circle around the fire who silently left his place and crept away, hanging his head in shame.

[Action 1 – Physical/Thoughts] This man was called Caedmon. He could not sing, and although he loved to listen to the songs of others, "whenever he saw the harp come near him," we are told, "he arose out of shame from the feast and went home to his house." Away from the bright firelight out into the lonely dark he crept with bent head and lagging steps. Perhaps he would stand a moment outside the door beneath the starlight and listen to the thunder of the waves and the shriek of the winds. And as he felt in his heart all the beauty and wonder of the world, the glory and the might of the sea and sky, he would ask in dumb pain why, when he could feel it touch his heart, he could not also sing of the beauty and wonder, glory and might.

[Action 2 – Physical/Dialogue] One night Caedmon crept away as usual, and went "out of the house where the entertainment was, to the stable, where he had to take care of the horses that night. He there composed himself to rest. A person appeared to him then in a dream and, calling him by name, said, 'Caedmon, sing some song to me.'

"He answered, 'I cannot sing; for that was the reason why I left the entertainment and retired to this place, because I cannot sing.'

"The other who talked to him replied, 'However, you shall sing.'

"'What shall I sing?' rejoined he.

"'Sing the beginning of created things,' said the other.

"Whereupon he presently began to sing verses to the praise of God, which he had never heard, the purport whereof was thus:—

'Now must we praise the guardian of heaven's kingdom,
The creator's might, and his mind's thought;
Glorious father of men! as of every wonder he,
Lord eternal, formed the beginning.
He first framed for the children of earth
The heaven as a roof; holy Creator!
Then mid-earth, the Guardian of mankind,
The eternal Lord, afterwards produced;
The earth for men, Lord almighty.'

"This," says the old historian, who tells the story in Latin, "is the sense, but not the words in order as he sang them in his sleep. For verses, though never so well composed, cannot be literally (that is word for word) translated out of one language into another without losing much of their beauty and loftiness."

Awakening from his sleep, Caedmon remembered all that he had sung in his dream. And the dream did not fade away as most dreams do. For he found that not only could he sing these verses, but he who had before been dumb and ashamed when the harp was put into his hand, could now make and sing more beautifully than could others. And all that he sang was to God's glory.

[Action 3 – Physical/Dialogue] In the morning, full of his wonderful new gift, Caedmon went to the steward who was set over him, and told him of the vision that he had had during the night. And the steward, greatly marveling, led Caedmon to the Abbess.

The Abbess listened to the strange tale. Then she commanded Caedmon, "in the presence of many learned men, to tell his dream and repeat the verses that they might all give their judgment what it was and whence his verse came."

So the simple farm laborer, who had no learning of any kind, sang while the learned and grave men listened. And he who was wont to creep away in dumb shame, fearing the laughter of his fellows, sang now with such beauty and sweetness that they were all of one mind, saying that the Lord Himself had, of His heavenly grace, given to Caedmon this new power.

[Action 4 – Physical] Then these learned men repeated to Caedmon some part of the Bible, explained the meaning of it, and asked him to tell it again in poetry. This Caedmon undertook to do, and when he fully understood the words, he went away. Next morning he returned and repeated all that he had been told, but now it was in beautiful poetry.

Then the Abbess saw that, indeed, the grace of God had come upon the man. She made him at once give up the life of a servant which he had been leading, and bade him become a monk. Caedmon gladly did her bidding, and when he had been received among them, his brother monks taught to him all the Bible stories.

But Caedmon could neither read nor write, nor is it at all likely that he ever learned to do either even after he became a monk, for we are told that "he was well advanced in years" before his great gift of song came to him. It is quite certain that he could not read Latin, so that all that he put into verse had to be taught to him by some more learned brother. And some one, too, must have written down the verses which Caedmon sang.

[Action 5 – Physical] We can imagine the pious, humble monk listening while another read and translated to him out of some Latin missal. He would sit with clasped hands and earnest eyes, intent on understanding. Then, when he had filled his mind with the sacred story, he would go away by himself and weave it into song. Perhaps he would walk about beneath the glowing stars or by the sounding sea, and thank God that he was no longer dumb, and that at last he could say forth all that before had been shut within his heart in an agony of silence. "And," we are told, "his songs and his verse were so winsome to hear, that his teachers themselves wrote and learned from his mouth."

"Thus Caedmon, keeping in mind all he heard, and, as it were, chewing the cud, converted the same into most harmonious verse; and sweetly repeating the same, made his masters in their turn his hearers.

"He sang the creation of the world, the origin of man, and all the history of Genesis; and made many verses on the departure of the children of Israel out of Egypt, and their entering into the land of promise, with many other histories from holy writ."

[Author's Comment] As has been said, there are lines in Beowulf which seem to have been written by a Christian. But all that is Christian in it is merely of the outside; it could easily be taken away, and the poem would remain perfect. The whole feeling of the poem is not Christian, but pagan. So it would seem that what is Christian in it has been added long after the poem was first made, yet added before the people had forgotten their pagan ways.

[Epilogue] For very long after they became Christian the Saxons kept their old pagan ways of thought, and Caedmon, when he came to sing of holy things, sang as a minstrel might. To him Abraham and Moses, and all the holy men of old, were like the warrior chieftains whom he knew and of whom the minstrels sang. And God to him was but the greatest of these warriors. He is "Heaven's Chief," "the Great Prince." The clash and clang of sword and trumpet calls are heard "amid the grim clash of helms." War filled the greatest half of life. All history, all poetry were bound up in it. Caedmon sang of what he saw, of what he knew. He was Christian, he had learned the lesson of peace on earth, but he lived amid the clash of arms and sang them.

❧

Lesson 15.1

Prose & Poetry

LITERARY ELEMENTS

1 **Read** *As you read with your students, discuss the footnote about the use of quotation marks. These conventions (single mark for a quote inside a quote, and no quotation mark at the end of a paragraph if the quotation continues into the next) are still in use in modern style guides like APA and Chicago Manual of Style.*

3 **Observe the Invention and Arrangement**
  ◆ **Lyrical Elements**
    ▪ Describes
    ▪ Senses
    ▪ Comparisons

  ◆ **Narrative Elements**
    ▪ **Setting** England during the second half of the seventh century A.D. (sometime between 657-680, dated by the time of Hilda's tenure as Abbess)
    ▪ **Characters** Britons, Saxons, Abbess Hilda, Caedmon, monks, learned men

- **Conflict** Caedmon is embarrassed by his musical inability
- **Resolution** God miraculously gifts the Caedmon with the ability to write and sing beautiful hymns.
- **Point of View** third person, limited omniscience ("Perhaps he would stand . . .") retelling the story from Bede's original version. *To apply this lesson further, look back at the narratives (including poems) which we have studied so far. Analyze the point of view of each one.*

4 Investigate the Context
- ◆ Identify the poem's **Literary Genre**
    - **Genre by literary period** – Early 20th century British
    - **Genre by poetic/narrative category** – non-fiction according to author's (Bede's) purpose. Henrietta Marshall is tracing the literary legacy of the British Isles, and demonstrating the beauty of Bede's narrative.

5 Connect the Thoughts
- ◆ Other miracle stories from Bede; miracle stories from missionaries who reach new peoples with the gospel

Lesson 15.2

Prose & Poetry

NARRATIVE PLOT ANALYSIS

See suggested scene divisions in selection at beginning of this lesson. Remember that answers may vary.

Eloquent Expression

COPIA OF CONSTRUCTION: COMBINING WITH CONJUNCTIONS

Answers will vary: 1. Caedmon could not sing, but he loved to listen to the songs of others, and he listened with great enjoyment. 2. The steward, the Abbess, and the learned men all listened to his song in astonishment.

Lesson 15.3

Language Logic

SENTENCE DIAGRAMMING AND PARSING

[Whenever he saw the harp come (near him,)] [he arose (out of shame) (from the feast) and went home (to his house.)]   *— complex sentence*

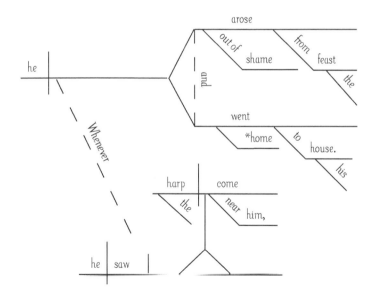

Home is an adverbial noun here. See Sentence Sense – Modifiers: Adverbial Nouns

WORD	PART OF SPEECH	DEFINE	CLASSIFY	PROPERTIES	FUNCTION
Whenever	conjunction	relates two clauses	--	--	introduces adverbial clause
near him	prepositional phrase	relates *him* to *come*	--	--	adverbial, modifying *come*
arose	verb	action	intransitive	3rd singular past	main verb in principal clause
his	pronoun	*Caedmon*	personal	3rd singular masculine	shows possession

Eloquent Expression

COPIA OF CONSTRUCTION: COMBINING WITH PARTICIPLES

Answers will vary: 1. A person appearing to Caedmon in a dream called him by name and told him to sing. 2. Leaving the bright firelight, Caedmon crept into the lonely dark with bent head and lagging steps.

Lesson 15.4

Eloquent Expression

COPIA OF CONSTRUCTION: COMBINING BY CLASS – COMPOUND

Answers will vary: 1. Caedmon sang about the creation of the world, he sang about the origin of man, and he sang about the land of promise. 2. Caedmon kept in mind all he heard and converted the same into harmonious verse, so he made his masters his hearers.

Lesson 15.5

Eloquent Expression

LITERARY IMITATION

[(On stormy nights,) [when the wind shook the four corners (of the house,)] and [the surf roared (along the cove) and (up the cliffs,)] I would see him (in a thousand forms,) and (with a thousand diabolical expressions.)]   – *compound-complex sentence*

Figure of description: anemographia; Figures of speech: personification – wind shook, surf roared

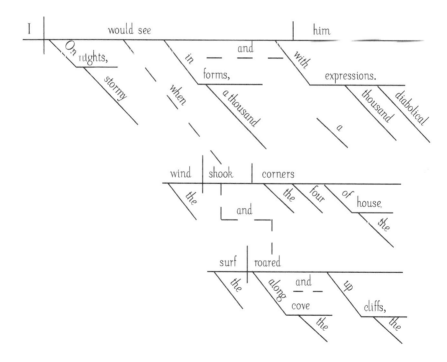

Lesson 16

❧

THE DIVINE GIFT OF SONG

The ECCLESIASTICAL HISTORY OF THE ENGLISH PEOPLE by Bede

There was in the monastery of this abbess a certain brother, marked in a special manner by the grace of God, for he was wont to make songs of piety and religion, so that whatever was expounded to him out of Scripture, he turned ere long into verse expressive of much sweetness and penitence, in English, which was his native language. By his songs the minds of many were often fired with contempt of the world, and desire of the heavenly life. Others of the English nation after him attempted to compose religious poems, but none could equal him, for he did not learn the art of poetry from men, neither was he taught by man, but by God's grace he received the free gift of song, for which reason he never could compose any trivial or vain poem, but only those which concern religion it behoved his religious tongue to utter. For having lived in the secular habit till he was well advanced in years, he had never learned anything of versifying; and for this reason sometimes at a banquet, when it was agreed to make merry by singing in turn, if he saw the harp come towards him, he would rise up from table and go out and return home.

Once having done so and gone out of the house where the banquet was, to the stable, where he had to take care of the cattle that night, he there composed himself to rest at the proper time. Thereupon one stood by him in his sleep, and saluting him, and calling him by his name, said, "Cædmon, sing me something." But he answered, "I cannot sing, and for this cause I left the banquet and retired hither, because I could not sing." Then he who talked to him replied, "Nevertheless thou must needs sing to me." "What must I sing?" he asked. "Sing the beginning of creation," said the other. Having received this answer he straightway began to sing verses to the praise of God the Creator, which he had never heard, the purport whereof was after this manner: "Now must we praise the Maker of the heavenly kingdom, the power of the Creator and His counsel, the deeds of the Father of glory. How He, being the eternal God, became the Author of all wondrous works, Who being the Almighty Guardian of the human race, first created heaven for the sons of men to be the covering of their dwelling place, and next the earth." This is the sense but not the order of the words as he sang them in his sleep; for verses, though never so well composed, cannot be literally translated out of one language into another without loss of their beauty and loftiness. Awaking from his sleep, he remembered all that he had sung in his dream, and soon added more after the same manner, in words which worthily expressed the praise of God.

In the morning he came to the reeve who was over him, and having told him of the gift he had received, was conducted to the abbess, and bidden, in the presence of many learned men, to tell his dream, and repeat the verses, that they might all examine and give their judgement upon the nature and origin of the gift whereof he spoke. And they all judged that heavenly grace had been granted to him by the Lord. They expounded to him a passage of sacred history or doctrine, enjoining upon him, if he could, to put it into verse. Having undertaken this task, he went away, and returning the next morning, gave them the passage he had been bidden to translate, rendered in most excellent verse. Whereupon the abbess, joyfully recognizing the grace of God in the man, instructed him to quit the secular habit, and take upon him monastic vows; and having received him into the monastery, she and all her people admitted him to the company of the brethren, and ordered that he should be taught the whole course of sacred history. So he, giving ear to all that he could learn, and bearing it in mind, and as it were ruminating, like a clean animal, turned it into most harmonious verse; and sweetly singing it, made his masters in their turn his hearers. He sang the creation of the world, the origin of man, and all the history of Genesis, the departure of the children of Israel out of Egypt, their entrance into the promised land, and many other histories from Holy Scripture; the Incarnation, Passion, Resurrection of our Lord, and His Ascension into heaven; the coming of the Holy Ghost, and the teaching of the Apostles; likewise he made many songs concerning the terror of future judgement, the horror of the pains of hell, and the joys of heaven; besides many more about the blessings and the judgements of God, by all of which he endeavoured to draw men away from the love of sin, and to excite in them devotion to well-doing and perseverance therein. For he was a very religious man, humbly submissive to the discipline of monastic rule, but inflamed with fervent zeal against those who chose to do otherwise; for which reason he made a fair ending of his life.

For when the hour of his departure drew near, it was preceded by a bodily infirmity under which he laboured for the space of fourteen days, yet it was of so mild a nature that he could talk and go about the whole time. In his neighbourhood was the house to which those that were sick, and like to die, were wont to be carried. He desired the person that ministered to him, as the evening came on of the night in which he was to depart this life, to make ready a place there for him to take his rest. The man, wondering why he should desire it, because there was as yet no sign of his approaching death, nevertheless did his bidding. When they had lain down there, and had been conversing happily and pleasantly for some time with those that were in the house before, and it was now past midnight, he asked them, whether they had the Eucharist within? They answered, "What need of the Eucharist? for you are not yet appointed to die, since you talk so merrily with us, as if you were in good health." "Nevertheless," said he, "bring me the Eucharist." Having received It into his hand, he asked, whether they were all in charity with him, and had no complaint against him, nor any quarrel or grudge. They answered, that they were all in perfect charity with him, and free from all anger; and in their turn they asked him to be of the same mind towards them. He answered at once, "I am in charity, my children, with all the servants of God." Then strengthening himself with the heavenly Viaticum, he prepared for the entrance into another life, and asked how near the time was when the brothers should be awakened to sing the nightly praises of the Lord? They answered, "It is not far off." Then he said, "It is well, let us await that hour;" and signing himself with the sign of the Holy Cross, he laid his head on the pillow, and falling into a slumber for a little while, so ended his life in silence.

Thus it came to pass, that as he had served the Lord with a simple and pure mind, and quiet devotion, so he now departed to behold His Presence, leaving the world by a quiet death; and that tongue, which had uttered so many wholesome words in praise of the Creator, spake its last words also in His praise, while he signed himself with the Cross, and commended his spirit into His hands; and by what has been here said, he seems to have had foreknowledge of his death.

CR

Lesson 16.1

Prose & Poetry

LITERARY ELEMENTS

3 **Observe the Invention and Arrangement**
- ◆ **Narrative Elements** see Lesson 15; keep in mind Bede's purpose: showing the spread of the gospel in the British Isles
  - ■ **Point of View** 3rd person limited omniscience

4 **Investigate the Context**
- ◆ Identify the poem's **Literary Genre**
  - ■ **Genre by literary period** – 8th century Britain, originally written in Latin
  - ■ **Genre by poetic/narrative category** – non-fiction; keep in mind that Bede interviewed eyewitnesses and carefully recorded what they told him, contrary to what many secular (and some Christian) scholars would have us believe. His intention was to record a truthful account of these events. As always, bias cannot help but be a factor; however this is true of every non-fiction narrative outside of Scripture. You must decide for yourself if you should believe what Bede has recorded. Are there comtemporaneous accounts that dispute Bede's accounts? (In his introduction, he actually seems to indicate that people in his day were questioning his miracle

accounts, and he answers their criticism.) Further questions to consider: Do miracles occur? Had miracles ceased in Bede's day?

Language Logic

SENTENCE DIAGRAMMING AND PARSING

[So the simple farm laborer, [who had no learning (of any kind)], sang [while the learned and grave men listened.]]   — *complex sentence*

WORD	PART OF SPEECH	DEFINE	CLASSIFY	PROPERTIES	FUNCTION
So	conjunction	relates two elements	n/a	n/a	connects two sentences
farm	adjective	modifies a noun	n/a	n/a	modifies *laborer*
who	pronoun	stands in for *laborer*	relative	3rd singular masculine	subject of relative clause
learning	verbal	*to learn*	participial noun (gerund)	present	DO *had*
while	conjunction	connects two elements	n/a	n/a	connects principal and subordinate clauses
learned	verbal	*to learn*	participle	perfect	modifies *men*

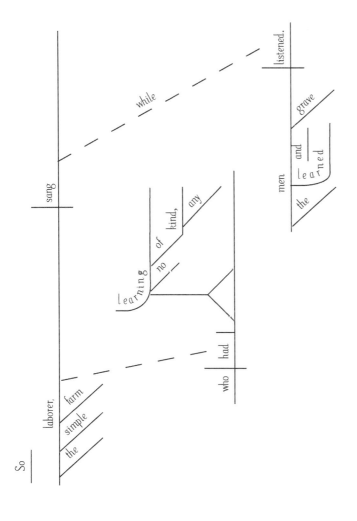

Lesson 16.2

Eloquent Expression

COPIA OF CONSTRUCTION: COMBINING BY CLASS: COMPLEX, COMPOUND-COMPLEX

Answers will vary: Complex: A person who called Caedmon by name appeared to him in a dream, and told him to sing. Compound-Complex: A person who called Caedmon by name appeared in a dream, and he told Caedmon to sing.

Lesson 16.3

Language Logic

SENTENCE DIAGRAMMING AND PARSING

[For he found [that not only could he sing these verses]], [but he [who had before been dumb and ashamed [when the harp was put into his hand]], could now make and sing beautifully.]

– compound-complex sentence

Nota Bene: *The clause starting with* but he... *is part of what he found, so it is classified here as a subordinate noun clause, not a principal clause. The relative pronoun* that *subordinates both clauses:* not only *and* but he

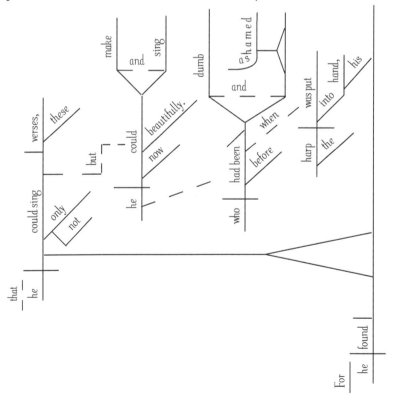

WORD	PART OF SPEECH	DEFINE	CLASSIFY	PROPERTIES	FUNCTION
dumb	adjective	modifies a pronoun	descriptive	--	predicate adjective modifying *who*
when	conjunc-tion	con-nects two clauses	--	--	connects principal and sub-ordinate clauses
harp	noun	thing	common	3rd singular neuter	subject of subordi-nate clause
beautifully	adverb	modifies a verb	--	--	modifies *sing*

Eloquent Expression

COPIA OF CONSTRUCTION: SWITCH SENTENCE CLASS BY FORM

1. Complex (one principal clause and one relative clause with one subject and two predicate verbs): [There was one among the circle around the fire] [who silently left his place and crept away, hanging his head in shame.]

2. Simple (Though this is a long sentence, it only has one subject, men. There are three compound verbs. A quick diagram will make this clear to the students.): These learned men repeated some part of the Bible to Caedmon, explained the meaning of it, and asked him to tell it again in poetry.

For rewrites, answers will vary: 1. Simple: There was one among the circle around the fire. He silently left his place and crept away, hanging his head in shame. Compound: There was one among the circle around the fire, and he left his place and crept away, hanging his head in shame. Compound-Complex: There was one among the circle around the fire who silently left his place and crept away, and he hung his head in shame.

2. Compound: These learned men repeated some part of the Bible to Caedmon, and they explained the meaning of it, and asked him to tell it again in poetry. Complex: These learned men repeated some part of the Bible to Caedmon, explaining the meaning of it, before they asked him to tell it again in poetry. Compound-Complex: These learned men repeated some part of the Bible to Caedmon, and they explained the meaning of it before they asked him to tell it again in poetry.

Lesson 17

❧

Caedmon's Hymn

Now [we] must honour the Guardian of heaven,
the might of the architect, and his purpose
the work of the Father of glory
as he, the eternal Lord, established the beginning of wonders;
he first created for the children of men
heaven as a roof, the holy creator
Then the Guardian of mankind,
the eternal Lord, afterwards appointed the middle earth,
the lands for me, the Lord almighty.

❧

Prose & Poetry

LITERARY ELEMENTS

3 Observe the Invention and Arrangement

- ◆ **Lyrical Elements**
  - He is describing and praising the "Guardian" and "Creator," along with His creation.
  - sight – envisioning the world with a roof (sky) and middle (earth)
  - Guardian – a keeper and guide for men
- ◆ **Narrative Elements**
  - **Point of View** 1st person

4 Investigate the Context

◆ Identify the poem's **Literary Genre**

- **Genre by literary period** – 8th century Britain, originally sung in the West Saxon tongue, but transcribed in Latin

- **Genre by poetic/narrative category** – lyrical

Lesson 17.2

Language Logic

SENTENCE DIAGRAMMING AND PARSING

[A person, (calling him by name), appeared (to him) then (in a dream) and told him (to sing some song.)]　　　　　　　　　　– *simple sentence*

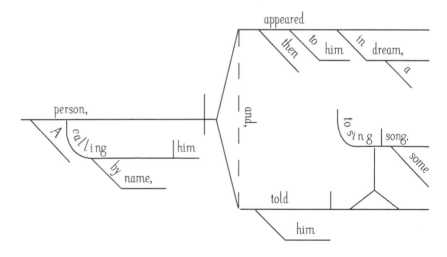

WORD	PART OF SPEECH	DEFINE	CLASSIFY	PROPERTIES	FUNCTION
appeared	verb	action	intransi-tive	3rd singular past	main verb of princi-pal clause

WORD	PART OF SPEECH	DEFINE	CLASSIFY	PROPERTIES	FUNCTION
calling	verbal	*to call*	participle	present	modifies *person*
him	pronoun	Caedmon	personal	3rd singular masculine	IO *calling*
song	noun	thing	common	3rd singular neuter	DO *told*

Lesson 17.3

Prose & Poetry

NARRATIVE SEQUENCE

The narrative arrangement for The Father of English Song *is linear, and in a sense could be considered ab ovo – from the "birth" of the church in the British Isles. The actual story of Caedmon does not begin at his birth, but near the action, so would be technically considered* in medias res, *then proceeds in a linear fashion to the end of the story.*

Lesson 17.4

Eloquent Expression

LITERARY IMITATION

[The forests had donned their sober brown and yellow, [while some trees (of the tenderer kind) had been nipped (by the frosts) (into brilliant dyes) (of orange, purple, and scarlet.)]]   *– complex sentence*

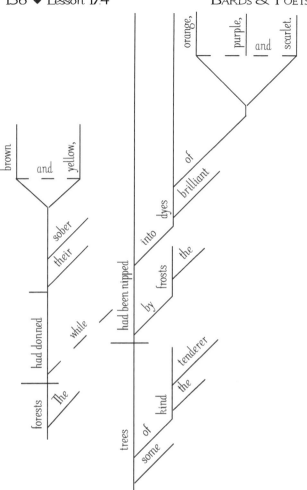

Nota Bene: *The original sentence reads:* The forests had put on their sober brown and yellow . . . *Our diagramming resources mostly agree that a colloquial verb phrase like* put on *should be diagrammed in a similar way to its equivalent* donned. *For this level, we thought it best to simplify the diagram so that students could more easily identify the verb and the direct objects. If you wish, you may explain this to your students and diagram the original sentence in class, with* put *as a transitive verb,* brown *and* yellow *as its objects, and* on *as an adverb. Also, note that* brown *and* yellow *here are substantive adjectives (brown leaves, yellow leaves), so we diagram them like the nouns they stand in for.*

Figure of description: chronographia

Figures of speech: personification *(had donned, had been nipped by frost)*

Lesson 18

❧

THE LORD'S MY SHEPHERD
The Scottish Psalter, 1650

The Lord's my Shepherd, I'll not want.
He makes me down to lie
In pastures green; He leadeth me
The quiet waters by.

My soul He doth restore again;
And me to walk doth make
Within the paths of righteousness,
Even for His own Name's sake.

Yea, though I walk in death's dark vale,
Yet will I fear no ill;
For Thou art with me; and Thy rod
And staff me comfort still.

My table Thou hast furnishèd
In presence of my foes;
My head Thou dost with oil anoint,
And my cup overflows.

Goodness and mercy all my life
Shall surely follow me;
And in God's house forevermore
My dwelling place shall be.

❧

Lesson 18.1

Prose & Poetry

LITERARY ELEMENTS

3 **Observe the Invention and Arrangement**
  - ◆ **Lyrical Elements**
    - The Lord as a shepherd
    - He makes you "see" quiet pastures, quiet waters, a dark valley, the shepherd's rod and staff, the well-stocked table and overflowing oil
    - He compares the Lord to a shepherd, and death to a dark valley

  - ◆ **Narrative Elements**
    - **Point of View** 1st person. Determining omniscience here could be theologically tricky. David would be limited, but God (the ultimate author of Scripture) is omniscient.

4 **Investigate the Context**
  - ◆ Identify the poem's **Literary Genre**
    - **Genre by literary period** – 17th century Scottish paraphrase of Psalm 23; for the Psalter
    - **Genre by poetic/narrative category** – lyrical

Language Logic

SENTENCE DIAGRAMMING AND PARSING

[My table Thou hast furnishèd
(In presence) (of my foes;)]
[My head Thou dost (with oil) anoint,]
And [my cup overflows.]   *– compound sentence*

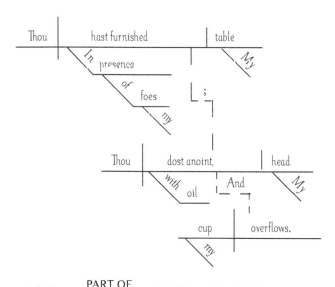

WORD	PART OF SPEECH	DEFINE	CLASSIFY	PROPERTIES	FUNCTION
table	noun	thing	common	3rd singular neuter	DO *hast furnished*
Thou	pronoun	stands in for *Lord*	personal	2nd singular masculine	subject of principal clause
hast furnished	verb	action	transitive	2nd singular present perfect	main verb of principal clause
In presence	prepositional phrase	relates *presence* to *hast furnished*	--	--	adverbial, modifying *hast furnished*

WORD	PART OF SPEECH	DEFINE	CLASSIFY	PROPERTIES	FUNCTION
And	conjunc-tion	con-nects two clauses	coordinate	--	connects two princi-pal clauses
my	pronoun	stands in for the narrator	personal	1st singular masculine	shows pos-session

Lesson 18.2

Prose & Poetry

METRICAL NOTATION: 8.6.8.6. – COMMON METER (CM).

Language Logic

THE INTERJECTION – HARVEY'S LESSON 151

I. Ha! laughest thou? 6. Oh, that the salvation of Israel were come out of Zion! 10. Soft! I did but dream! II. What! old acquaintance! could not all this flesh Keep in a little life? Poor Jack, farewell! I could have better spared a better man. — *Shakespeare.*

WORD	PART OF SPEECH	DEFINE	CLASSIFY	PROPERTIES	FUNCTION
1. Ha!	interjec-tion	shows sudden or strong emotion	--	--	indepen-dent ele-ment
6. Oh,	interjec-tion	shows sudden or strong emotion	--	--	
10. soft!	interjec-tion	shows sudden or strong emotion	--	--	

SENTENCE DIAGRAMMING

1. Hark! The clock strikes one.   *– simple sentence*

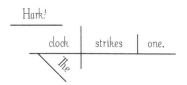

2. Oh, what a noble mind here is o'erthrown!   *– simple sentence*

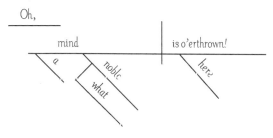

Lesson 18.3

Prose & Poetry

SCANSION AND ANALYSIS

Rhyme Scheme: ABCB

Stanza Name: Quatrain

Poetic Meter: Alternating lines of Iambic Tetrameter and Trimeter

| ᴗ ⁄ | ᴗ ⁄ | ᴗ ⁄ | ᴗ ⁄ |
The Lord's my Shep herd, I'll not want.

| ᴗ ⁄ | ᴗ ⁄ | ᴗ ⁄ |
He makes me down to lie

| ᴗ ⁄ | ᴗ ⁄ | ᴗ ⁄ | ᴗ ⁄ |
In pas tures green; He lead eth me

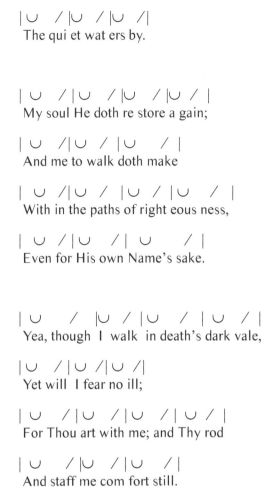

| ∪ / |∪ / |∪ /|
The qui et wat ers by.

| ∪ / |∪ / |∪ / |∪ / |
My soul He doth re store a gain;

| ∪ / |∪ / |∪ / |
And me to walk doth make

| ∪ / |∪ / |∪ / |∪ / |
With in the paths of right eous ness,

| ∪ / |∪ / | ∪ / |
Even for His own Name's sake.

| ∪ / |∪ / |∪ / | ∪ / |
Yea, though I walk in death's dark vale,

|∪ / |∪ / |∪ /|
Yet will I fear no ill;

| ∪ / |∪ / |∪ / |∪ / |
For Thou art with me; and Thy rod

| ∪ / |∪ / |∪ / |
And staff me com fort still.

Metrical Notation and Name for "Our God, Our Help In Ages Past": 8.6.8.6 – Common Meter (C.M.)

Language Logic

SENTENCE DIAGRAMMING

1. There is a fountain filled with blood drawn from Immanuel's veins.

   —Cowper   *– simple sentence*

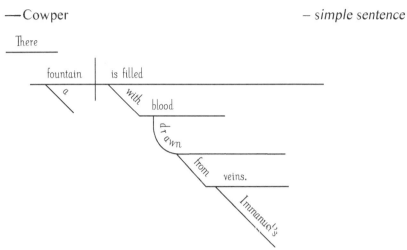

2. It is hard to be sure of anything among so many marvels. —Tolkien

– simple sentence

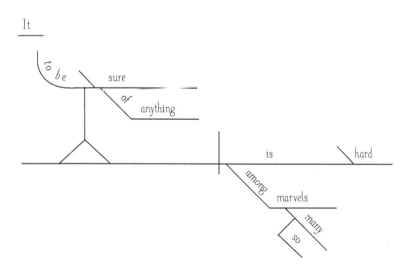

Eloquent Expression

FIGURES OF SPEECH – ANASTROPHE
Representative, not exhaustive.

Anastrophe in "The Lord's My Shepherd": He makes me down to lie = He makes me to lie down; He leadeth me the quiet waters by = He leadeth me by the quiet waters; My soul He doth restore = He doth restore my soul; Me to walk doth make = doth make me to walk; Yet will I fear no ill = Yet I will fear no ill; My table Thou hast furnished = Thou hast furnished my table; My head Thou dost with oil anoint = Thou dost anoint my head with oil; And in God's house forevermore my dwelling place shall be = My dwelling place shall be in God's house forevermore

Simile in "The Lord's My Shepherd": none

Metaphor in "The Lord's My Shepherd": Lord's my Shepherd, makes me down to lie in pastures green, He leadeth me the quiet waters by, within the paths of righteousness, death's dark vale.

The fourth verse is probably literal for David, and also metaphorical in the sense of God's provision of physical needs as well as a joyful heart, even in times of trouble.

Personification in "The Lord's My Shepherd": rod and staff me comfort still, goodness and mercy shall surely follow me

A few examples of anastrophe in other poems we have studied (there are many more!): "The Reading Mother" Richer than I you can never be; "The Land of Story-Books" Around the fire my parents sit; "A Book" This traverse may the poorest take;

Lesson 18.4

Prose & Poetry

SCANSION:

```
| ∪ /| ∪   / | ∪ /| ∪ /|
My ta ble Thou hast fur nish èd
```

```
|∪ /|  ∪ /| ∪ / |
In pres ence of my foes;
```

```
| ∪ / | ∪   / | ∪ /| ∪ / |
My head Thou dost with oil a noint,
```

```
|  ∪ / | ∪ /| ∪ /  |
And  my  cup o ver flows.
```

```
|  ∪   / | ∪   /| ∪ /| ∪ /|
Good ness and mer cy all my life
```

```
|  ∪   / | ∪ /|  ∪ /|
Shall sure ly fol low me;
```

```
|  ∪ /| ∪   /  | ∪ /| ∪ / |
And in God's house for ev er more
```

```
|∪   / | ∪ / | ∪ /|
My dwell ing place shall be.
```

Metrical Notation and Name for "A Mighty Fortress":

8.7.8.7.6.6.6.6.7 – no metrical name

Anastrophe in "A Mighty Fortress": A mighty fortress is our God = Our God is a mighty fortress; Our helper he = he (is) our helper

Eloquent Expression

LITERARY IMITATION

[Silently, (one by one), (in the infinite meadows) (of heaven,)

Blossomed the lovely stars, (the forget-me-nots of the angels.)]

– simple sentence

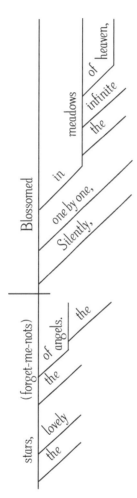

Figures of speech: metaphor – meadows of heaven, Blossomed the lovely stars, forget-me-nots of the angels; anastrophe – Blossomed the lovely stars

Figure of description: astrothesia (vivid description of the night sky)

Lesson 18.5

Prose & Poetry

METRICAL NOTATION AND NAME FOR "UNLESS THE HOUSE THE LORD SHALL BUILD": 8.8.8.8   LONG METER (L.M.)

Anastrophe in "Unless the House the Lord Shall Build": Just about every line in this hymn has anastrophe. A few examples in stanza 1: Unless the Lord the house shall build = Unless the Lord shall build the house; Unless the Lord the city shield = Unless the Lord shield the city; The guards a useless watch maintain = The guards maintain a useless watch.

Language Logic

SENTENCE DIAGRAMMING AND PARSING

Yea, [though I walk (in death's dark vale,)]
Yet [will I fear no ill;]
[For Thou art (with me;)] and [Thy rod
And staff me comfort still.]   – compound-complex sentence

Nota Bene: *We have marked and diagrammed* For *in the third line as a subordinate conjunction. In future books, students will discover that* for *is sometimes used as a coordinate conjunction, and sometimes as a subordinate conjunction, and they will learn how to distinguish which is which. This is true of a few other conjunctions as well. (See* Sentence Sense *7.3 and 7.4.) At this point, it is best to just tell students before they diagram that* For *in this sentence is a subordinate conjunction. If they diagram it on their own as a coordinate conjunction, you could point it out, but do not mark a student wrong for this.*

If you are curious, we classify For *as a causal subordinate conjunction, denoting condition or reason. This is where higher-level abstract thinking really comes into play, and the value of diagramming as an exercise in logic becomes very evident!*

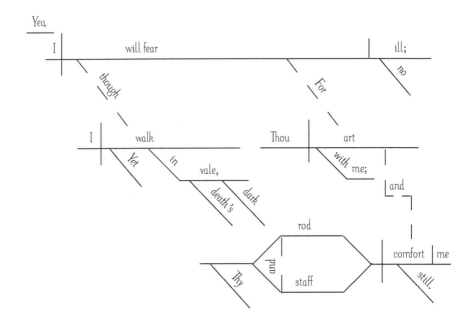

WORD	PART OF SPEECH	DEFINE	CLASSIFY	PROPERTIES	FUNCTION
Yet	adverb	modifies a verb	--	--	modifies *walk*
though	conjunc- tion	con- nects two clauses	subordi- nate	--	joins principal and sub- ordinate clauses
death's	noun	idea	common	3rd singular neuter (or masculine)	shows pos- session of *vale*
with me	prepo- sitional phrase	relates *me* to *art*	--	--	adverbial, modifying *art*
me (com- fort)	pronoun	stands in for the poet	personal	1st singular masculine	DO *com- fort*

Lesson 19

ℭℜ

THE CYCLOPS

from THE STORY OF THE ODYSSEY by Alfred Church

[Prologue] Then Ulysses answered the King, saying: "What shall I tell thee first, and what last, for many sorrows have the gods laid upon me? First, I will tell my name, that ye may know it, and that there may be friendship between us, even when I shall be far away. I am Ulysses, son of Laertes. In Ithaca I dwell. Many islands lie about it, but Ithaca is furthest to the west, and the others face the sun-rising. Very rugged is this island of Ithaca, but it is the mother of brave men; verily, there is nothing dearer to a man than his own country. Calypso, the fair goddess, would have had me abide with her, to be her husband; but she did not prevail, because there is nothing that a man loves more than his country and his parents. But now I will tell thee of all the troubles that the gods laid upon me as I journeyed from Troy.

[Action 1] "The wind that bare me from Troy brought me to Ismarus which is a city of the Cicones. This I sacked, slaying the people that dwelt therein. But the people of the city fetched their kinsmen that dwelt in the mountains, and they overcame us, and drave us to our ships. Six from each ship perished, but the remainder of us escaped from death.

[Action 2 – Place, Action] "Then we sailed, stricken with grief for our dear comrades, yet rejoicing that we had escaped from destruction. When we had sailed a little space, Zeus sent the north wind against us with a mighty storm, covering with clouds both land and sea, and the ships were driven before it. So we lowered the sails, and rowed the ships to the land with all our might. For two days we endured much distress and sorrow, but on the third, when the morning light appeared, we hoisted the sails and rested. Then I should have come to my own country, but the north wind and the sea drave me from my course. For nine days did the wind carry us before it.

[Action 3 – place, action, person, time] "And on the tenth day we came to the land where the lotus grows—a wondrous fruit, for

whoever eats of it cares not to see country or wife or children again.
Now the Lotus-eaters, for so the people of the land are called, were a
kindly folk, and gave of the fruit to some of the sailors, not meaning
them any harm, but thinking it to be the best that they had to give.
These, when they had eaten, said that they would not sail any more
over the sea; and, when I heard this, I bade their comrades bind them
and carry them, sadly complaining, to the ships.

[Action 4 − Place, Action] "Then, the wind having abated,
we took to our oars, and rowed for many days till we came to the
country where the Cyclopes dwell. Now a mile or so from the shore
there was an island, very fair and fertile, but no man dwells there or
tills the soil, and in the island a harbour where a ship may be safe
from all winds, and at the head of the harbour a stream falling from
a rock, and whispering alders all about it. Into this the ships passed
safely, and were hauled up on the beach, and the crews slept by them,
waiting for the morning.

[Action 5 − Place, Time, Action] "When the dawn appeared,
we wandered through the island; and the Nymphs of the land started
the wild goats, that my company might have food to eat. Thereupon
we took our bows and our spears from the ships, and shot at the
goats; and the gods gave us plenty of prey. Twelve ships I had in my
company, and each ship had nine goats for its share, and my own
portion was ten.

"Then all the day we sat and feasted, drinking sweet wine which
we had taken from the city of the Cicones, and eating the flesh of
the goats; and as we sat we looked across to the land of the Cyclops,
seeing the smoke and hearing the voices of the men and of the sheep
and of the goats. And when the sun set and darkness came over the
land, we lay down upon the seashore and slept.

[Action 6 − Place, Time, Action] "The next day I gathered my
men together, and said, 'Abide ye here, dear friends; I with my own
ship and my own company will go and find whether the folk that
dwell in yonder island are just or unjust.'

"So I climbed into my ship, and bade my company follow me: so
we came to the land of the Cyclops. Close to the shore was a cave,
with laurels round about the mouth. This was the dwelling of the
Cyclops. Alone he dwelt, a creature without law. Nor was he like to
mortal men, but rather to some wooded peak of the hills that stands
out apart from all the rest.

[Action 7 – Place, Action] "Then I bade the rest of my comrades abide by the ship, and keep it, but I took twelve men, the bravest that there were in the crew, and went forth. I had with me a goat-skin full of the wine, dark red, and sweet, which the priest of Apollo at Ismarus had given me. So precious was it that none in his house knew of it saving himself and his wife. When they drank of it they mixed twenty measures of water with one of wine, and the smell that went up from it was wondrous sweet. No man could easily refrain from drinking it. With this wine I filled a great skin and bore it with me; also I bare corn in a pouch, for my heart within me told me that I should need it.

"So we entered the cave, and judged that it was the dwelling of some rich and skilful shepherd. For within there were pens for the young of the sheep and of the goats, divided all according to their age, and there were baskets full of cheeses, and full milkpails ranged along the wall. But the Cyclops himself was away in the pastures. Then my companions besought me that I would depart, taking with me, if I would, a store of cheeses and some of the lambs and of the kids. But I would not, for I wished to see what manner of host this strange shepherd might be, and, if it might be, to take a gift from his hand, such as is the due of strangers. Verily, his coming was not to be a joy to my company.

[Action 8 – Time, Action, Person] "It was evening when the Cyclops came home, a mighty giant, very tall of stature, and when we saw him we fled into the cave in great fear. On his shoulder he bore a vast bundle of pine logs for his fire, and threw them down outside the cave with a great crash, and drove the flocks within, and closed the entrance with a huge rock, which twenty wagons and more could not bear. Then he milked the ewes and all the she-goats, and half of the milk he curdled for cheese, and half he set ready for himself, when he should sup. Next he kindled a fire with the pine logs, and the flame lighted up all the cave, showing to him both me and my comrades.

"'Who are ye?' cried Polyphemus, for that was the giant's name. 'Are ye traders or pirates?'

"I shuddered at the dreadful voice and shape, but bare me bravely, and answered: 'We are no pirates, mighty sir, but Greeks sailing back from Troy, and subjects of the great King Agamemnon, whose fame is spread from one end of heaven to the other. And we are come to beg hospitality of thee in the name of Zeus, who rewards or punishes hosts and guests according as they be faithful the one to the other, or no.'

"'Nay,' said the giant; 'it is but idle talk to tell me of Zeus and the other gods. We Cyclopes take no account of gods, holding ourselves to be much better and stronger than they. But come, tell me where have you left your ship?'

"But I saw his thought when he asked about the ship, for he was minded to break it, and take from us all hope of flight. Therefore I answered him craftily:—

"Ship have we none, for that which was ours King Poseidon brake, driving it on a jutting rock on this coast, and we whom thou seest are all that are escaped from the waves."

[Action 9 — Physical] "Polyphemus answered nothing, but without more ado caught up two of the men, as a man might catch up the pups of a dog, and dashed them on the ground, and tare them limb from limb, and devoured them, with huge draughts of milk between, leaving not a morsel, not even the very bones. But we that were left, when we saw the dreadful deed, could only weep and pray to Zeus for help. And when the giant had filled his maw with human flesh and with the milk of the flocks, he lay down among his sheep and slept.

[Action 10 — Physical] "Then I questioned much in my heart whether I should slay the monster as he slept, for I doubted not that my good sword would pierce to the giant's heart, mighty as he was. But my second thought kept me back, for I remembered that if I should slay him, I and my comrades would yet perish miserably. For who could move away the great rock that lay against the door of the cave? So we waited till the morning, with grief in our hearts. And the monster woke, and milked his flocks, and afterwards, seizing two men, devoured them for his meal. Then he went to the pastures, but put the great rock on the mouth of the cave, just as a man puts down the lid upon his quiver.

[Action 11 — Time, Action] "All that day I was thinking what I might best do to save myself and my companions, and the end of my thinking was this. There was a mighty pole in the cave, green wood of an olive tree, big as a ship's mast, which Polyphemus purposed to use, when the smoke should have dried it, as a walking-staff. Of this I cut off a fathom's length, and my comrades sharpened it and hardened it in the fire, and then hid it away. [Action 12 – time, action] At evening the giant came back, and drove his sheep into the cave, nor left the rams outside, as he had been wont to do before, but shut them in. And having duly done his shepherd's work, he took, as before, two of my comrades, and devoured them. And when he had finished his supper, I came forward, holding the wine-skin in my hand, and said:—

"'Drink, Cyclops, now that thou hast feasted. Drink, and see what precious things we had in our ship. But no one hereafter will come to thee with such, if thou dealest with strangers as cruelly as thou hast dealt with us.'

"Then the Cyclops drank, and was mightily pleased, and said: 'Give me again to drink, and tell me thy name, stranger, and I will give thee a gift such as a host should give. In good truth this is a rare liquor. We, too, have vines, but they bear not wine like this, which, indeed, must be such as the gods drink in heaven.'

"Then I gave him the cup again, and he drank. Thrice I gave it to him, and thrice he drank, not knowing what it was, and how it would work within his brain.

"Then I spake to him: 'Thou didst ask my name, Cyclops. My name is No Man. And now that thou knowest my name, thou shouldest give me thy gift.'

"And he said: 'My gift shall be that I will eat thee last of all thy company.'

[Action 13 – Physical, Time] "And as he spake, he fell back in a drunken sleep. Then I bade my comrades be of good courage, for the time was come when they should be delivered. And they thrust the stake of olive wood into the fire till it was ready, green as it was, to burst into flame, and they thrust it into the monster's eye; for he had but one eye and that was in the midst of his forehead, with the eyebrow below it. And I, standing above, leaned with all my force upon the stake, and turned it about, as a man bores the timber of a ship with a drill. And the burning wood hissed in the eye, just as the red-hot iron hisses in the water when a man seeks to temper steel for a sword.

[Action 14 – Physical] "Then the giant leapt up, and tore away the stake, and cried aloud, so that all the Cyclopes who dwelt on the mountain-side heard him and came about his cave, asking him: 'What aileth thee, Polyphemus, that thou makest this uproar in the peaceful night, driving away sleep? Is any one robbing thee of thy sheep, or seeking to slay thee by craft or force?' And the giant answered, 'No Man slays me by craft.'

"'Nay, but,' they said, 'if no man does thee wrong, we cannot help thee. The sickness which great Zeus may send, who can avoid? Pray to our father, Poseidon, for help.'

"So they spake, and I laughed in my heart when I saw how I had deceived them by the name that I had given.

[Action 15 – Physical] "But the Cyclops rolled away the great stone from the door of the cave, and sat in the midst, stretching out his hands, to feel whether perchance the men within the cave would seek to go out among the sheep.

"Long did I think how I and my comrades should best escape. At last I lighted upon a plan that seemed better than all the rest, and much I thanked Zeus because this once the giant had driven the rams with the other sheep into the cave. For, these being great and strong, I fastened my comrades under the bellies of the beasts, tying them with willow twigs, of which the giant made his bed. One ram I took, and fastened a man beneath it, and two others I set, one on either side. So I did with the six, for but six were left out of the twelve who had ventured with me from the ship. And there was one mighty ram, far larger than all the others, and to this I clung, grasping the fleece tight with both my hands. So we all waited for the morning. [Action 16 – Time, Action] And when the morning came, the rams rushed forth to the pasture; but the giant sat in the door and felt the back of each as it went by, nor thought to try what might be underneath. Last of all went the great ram. And the Cyclops knew him as he passed, and said:—

"'How is this, thou who art the leader of the flock? Thou art not wont thus to lag behind. Thou hast always been the first to run to the pastures and streams in the morning, and the first to come back to the fold when evening fell; and now thou art last of all. Perhaps thou art troubled about thy master's eye, which some wretch—No Man, they call him—has destroyed. He has not escaped, and I would that thou couldest speak, and tell me where he is lurking. Of a truth, I would dash out his brains upon the ground, and avenge me on this No Man.'

"So speaking, he let the ram pass out of the cave. [Action 17 — place, action] But when we were now out of reach of the giant, I loosed my hold of the ram, and then unbound my comrades. And we hastened to our ship, not forgetting to drive the sheep before us, and often looking back till we came to the seashore. Right glad were those that had abode by the ship to see us. Nor did they lament for those that had died, though we were fain to do so, for I forbade, fearing lest the noise of their weeping should betray where we were to the giant. Then we all climbed into the ship, and sitting well in order on the benches smote the sea with our oars, laying to right lustily, that we might the sooner get away from the accursed land. And when we had rowed a hundred yards or so, so that a man's voice could yet be heard by one who stood upon the shore, I stood up in the ship and shouted:—

"'He was no coward, O Cyclops, whose comrades thou didst so foully slay in thy den. Justly art thou punished, monster, that devourest thy guests in thy dwelling. May the gods make thee suffer yet worse things than these!'

[Action 18 — Physical] "Then the Cyclops in his wrath brake off the top of a great hill, a mighty rock, and hurled it where he had heard the voice. Right in front of the ship's bow it fell, and a great wave rose as it sank, and washed the ship back to the shore. But I seized a long pole with both hands, and pushed the ship from the land, and bade my comrades ply their oars, nodding with my head, for I would not speak, lest the Cyclops should know where we were. Then they rowed with all their might and main.

"And when we had gotten twice as far as before, I made as if I would speak again; but my comrades sought to hinder me, saying: 'Nay, my lord, anger not the giant any more. Surely we thought before that we were lost, when he threw the great rock, and washed our ship back to the shore. And if he hear thee now, he may still crush our ship and us.'

"But I would not be persuaded, but stood up and said: 'Hear, Cyclops! If any man ask who blinded thee, say that it was the warrior Ulysses, son of Laertes, dwelling in Ithaca.'

"And the Cyclops answered with a groan: 'Of a truth, the old prophecies are fulfilled; for long ago there came to this land a prophet who foretold to me that Ulysses would rob me of my sight. But I looked for a great and strong man, who should subdue me by force, and now a weakling has done the deed, having cheated me with wine.'

[Action19 — Physical] "Then the Cyclops lifted up his hands to Poseidon and prayed: 'Hear me, Poseidon, if I am indeed thy son and thou my father. May this Ulysses never reach his home! or, if the Fates have ordered that he should reach it, may he come alone, all his comrades lost, and come to find sore trouble in his house!'

"And as he ended, he hurled another mighty rock, which almost lighted on the rudder's end, yet missed it as by a hair's breadth. And the wave that it raised was so great that it bare us to the other shore.

[Action 20 — Place, Time, Action] "So we came to the island of the wild goats, where we found our comrades, who, indeed, had waited long for us in sore fear lest we had perished. Then I divided amongst my company all the sheep which we had taken from the Cyclops. And all, with one consent, gave me for my share the great ram which had carried me out of the cave, and I sacrificed it to Zeus. And all that day we feasted right merrily on the flesh of sheep and on sweet wine, and when the night was come, we lay down upon the shore and slept.

Lesson 19.1

Prose & Poetry

LITERARY ELEMENTS

3 Observe the Invention and Arrangement
◆ Lyrical Elements

- Describes
- Senses
- Comparisons

◆ **Narrative Elements**

- **Setting** Ancient Greece, circa 1200 B.C

- **Characters** Ulysses, his crew, the Cyclops, the Cyclopes

- **Conflict** Ulysses and his men trapped in a cave with a man-eating monster

- **Resolution** Resourceful Odysseus devises a way to blind the Cyclops and escape.

- **Sequence** *in medias res*, told in a linear fashion some time after the events of the story

- **Point of View** First person limited. The overall narrative frame is third person, based on the opening sentence. But Ulysses's narrative itself is told in first.

4 Investigate the Context

◆ Identify the poem's **Literary Genre**

- **Genre by literary period** – original story, ancient Greece; retelling late 19th century English (Victorian)

- **Genre by poetic/narrative category** – Treat as non-fiction, with possible fictional details. See discussion in Teaching Helps, Lesson 7.1.

5 Connect the Thoughts

◆ Stories with similar plots, messages, or characters: other stories about Ulysses from the *Iliad* and the *Odyssey;* other stories of clever escapes.

Lesson 19.2

Prose & Poetry

NARRATIVE PLOT ANALYSIS

See suggested scene divisions in selection at beginning of this lesson. Remember that answers may vary. This is a lengthy selection, so we have instructed students to limit the number of scene divisions to between 15 and 25. This will require discrimination skills. Plan to work with your students on this assignment.

Eloquent Expression

COPIA OF CONSTRUCTION: WORDS, PHRASES, CLAUSES

Answers will vary: 1. Now the Lotus-Eaters were a folk of great kindness. Now the Lotus-Eaters were a folk who were kind 2. The Nymphs roused the goats running wild on the island. The Nymphs roused the goats which were running wild on the island. 3. Ulysses answered him with craft. Ulysses, who was crafty, answered him. 4. At this time, they should be delivered. When this was done, they should be delivered.

Lesson 19.3

Eloquent Expression

SENTENCE DIAGRAMMING AND PARSING

[(On his shoulder (he bore a vast bundle (of pine logs) (for his fire), and threw them down (outside the cave) (with a great crash), and drove the flocks within, and closed the entrance (with a huge rock),] [which twenty wagons and more could not bear.]   *— complex sentence*

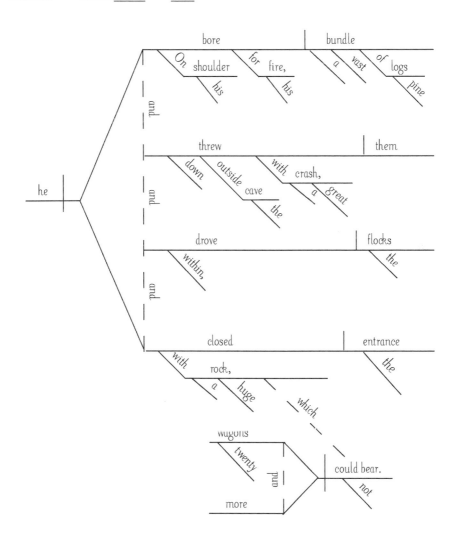

WORD	PART OF SPEECH	DEFINE	CLASSIFY	PROPERTIES	FUNCTION
bore	verb	action	transitive	3rd singular past	main verb in principal clause
with a great crash	prepositional phrase	relates *crash* to *threw*	--	--	adverbial, modifying *threw*
entrance	noun	place (or thing)	common	3rd singular neuter	DO *closed*
which	pronoun	*rock*	relative	3rd singular neuter	relative pronoun only (no other function in clause)
more	adjective	modifies implied *wagons*	definitive	--	used substantively as a noun subject

Eloquent Expression

COPIA OF CONSTRUCTION: CLAUSE PLACEMENT

Answers will vary: 1. I had with me a goat-skin, which the priest of Apollo at Ismarus had given me, full of the wine, dark red and sweet. 2. I came forward when he had finished his supper, holding the wine-skin in my hand.

Lesson 19.4

Eloquent Expression

COPIA OF CONSTRUCTION: ADJECTIVE AND ADVERB ELEMENTS

Answers will vary: 1. If I should slay him, I and my comrades, miserable, would perish. If I should slay him, I and my comrades would perish in great misery. 2. Then the Cyclops, who was full of wrath, brake off the top of a great hill and hurled it down. Then the Cyclops wrathfully brake off the top of a great hill and hurled it down.

Lesson 19.5

Eloquent Expression

LITERARY IMITATION

[Sing in me, Muse, and (through me) tell the story
(of that man) skilled (in all ways) (of contending,)
the wanderer, harried (for years) (on end,)]
[after he plundered the stronghold
(on the proud height) (of Troy.)]   — *complex sentence*

Figure of description: none

Figures of speech: personification — Muse, proud height

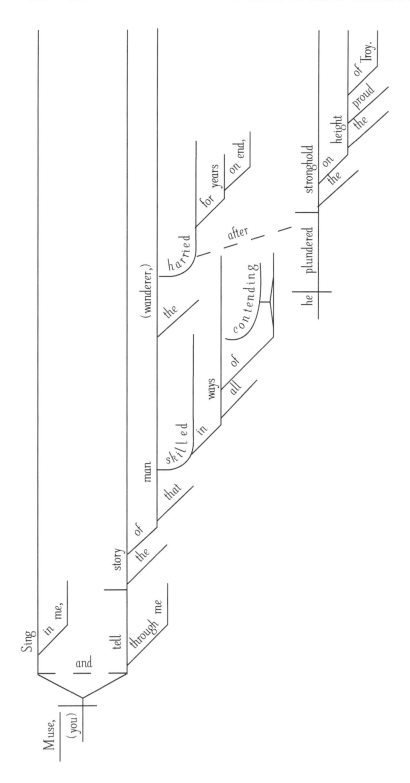

Lesson 20

❧

from THE ODYSSEY OF HOMER

Translated by Alexander Pope

Now did the rosy-fingered morn arise,
And shed her sacred light along the skies;
He wakes, he lights the fire, he milks the dams,
And to the mother's teats submits the lambs.
The task thus finish'd of his morning hours,
Two more he snatches, murders, and devours.
Then pleased, and whistling, drives his flock before,
Removes the rocky mountain from the door,
And shuts again: with equal ease disposed,
As a light quiver's lid is oped and closed.
His giant voice the echoing region fills:
His flocks, obedient, spread o'er all the hills.
"Thus left behind, even in the last despair
I thought, devised, and Pallas heard my prayer.
Revenge, and doubt, and caution, work'd my breast;
But this of many counsels seem'd the best:
The monster's club within the cave I spied,
A tree of stateliest growth, and yet undried,
Green from the wood: of height and bulk so vast,
The largest ship might claim it for a mast.
This shorten'd of its top, I gave my train
A fathom's length, to shape it and to plane;
The narrower end I sharpen'd to a spire,
Whose point we harden'd with the force of fire,
And hid it in the dust that strew'd the cave,
Then to my few companions, bold and brave,
Proposed, who first the venturous deed should try,
In the broad orbit of his monstrous eye
To plunge the brand and twirl the pointed wood,
When slumber next should tame the man of blood.
Just as I wished, the lots were cast on four:

Myself the fifth. We stand and wait the hour.
He comes with evening: all his fleecy flock
Before him march, and pour into the rock:
Not one, or male or female, stayed behind
(So fortune chanced, or so some god designed);
Then heaving high the stone's unwieldy weight,
He roll'd it on the cave and closed the gate.

☙❧

Lesson 20.1

Prose & Poetry

LITERARY ELEMENTS

3 Observe the Invention and Arrangement
- ◆ **Lyrical Elements**
  - ▪ He describes morning, the log, and the activities of the Cyclops.
  - ▪ Sense of sight, hearing
  - ▪ He compares morning to a person.

- ◆ **Narrative Elements** see Lesson 19.1
  - ▪ **Point of View** 1st person limited (for this selection)

4 Investigate the Context
- ◆ Identify the poem's **Literary Genre**
  - ▪ **Genre by literary period** – early 18th century poetic retelling of ancient Greek epic
  - ▪ **Genre by poetic/narrative category** – narrative

SCANSION

The meter is iambic pentameter, and it is arranged in rhyming couplets (no stanza form per se).

Lesson 20.2

Language Logic

SENTENCE DIAGRAMMING AND PARSING

[I answered him craftily,] ["Ship have we none, for that [which was ours] King Poseidon brake, driving it (on a jutting rock) (on this coast.")]

– compound-complex sentence

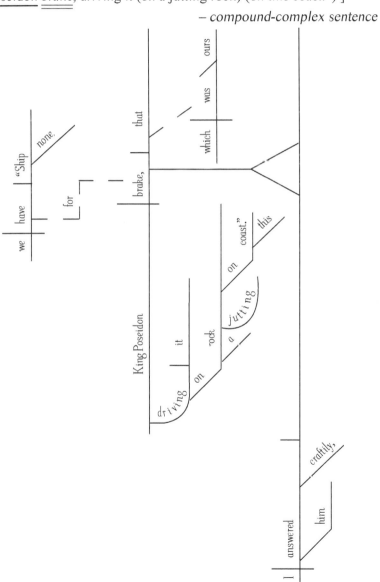

Notice the anastrophe: Ship have we none . . .

WORD	PART OF SPEECH	DEFINE	CLASSIFY	PROPERTIES	FUNCTION
him	pronoun	*Cyclops*	personal	3rd singular masculine	IO *answered*
none	adjective	modifies a noun	definitive	--	modifies *Ship*
that	adjective	modifies a (miss-ing) noun	definitive	--	used sub-stantively as DO *brake*
driving	verbal	*to drive*	participle	present	modi-fies *King Poseidon*
jutting	verbal	*to jut*	participle	present	modifies *rocks*

Eloquent Expression

COPIA OF CONSTRUCTION: PRINCIPAL AND SUBORDINATE CLAUSES

Answers will vary: 1. We had sailed a little space before Zeus sent the north wind against us with a mighty storm. 2. The Cyclopes who dwelt on the mountain-side heard him when the giant leapt up and cried aloud.

Lesson 20.3

Prose & Poetry

Nota Bene: *Search online for a tutorial on tips for making outlines in your particular word-processing program if you need help with this.*

Language Logic

SENTENCE DIAGRAMMING AND PARSING

[The giant said [it was but idle talk to tell him (of Zeus and
the other gods)], as [the Cyclopes take no account (of gods.)]]

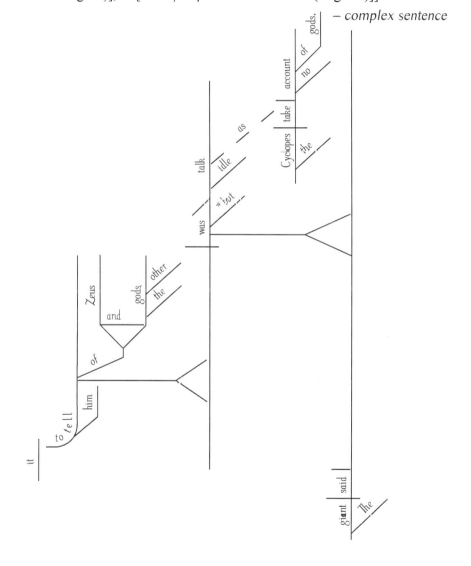

— complex sentence

*But *means* only or merely *in context of the sentence; the dictionary says
this is its adverbial meaning. We determine a word's part of speech according
to its meaning within the sentence, so the dictionary is a vital resource for
diagramming!*

WORD	PART OF SPEECH	DEFINE	CLASSIFY	PROPERTIES	FUNCTION
but	adverb	modifies a verb	--	--	modifies *was*
talk	noun	idea	common	3rd singular neuter	predicate nominative
Zeus	noun	person	proper	3rd singular masculine	OP *of*
as	conjunc-tion	con-nects two clauses	subordi-nate	--	subordinat-ing only, no role in clause
gods	noun	person	common	3rd singular common	OP *of*

Eloquent Expression

COPIA OF CONSTRUCTION: DIRECT AND INDIRECT QUOTATIONS

Answers will vary: 1. The Cyclops demanded that Odysseus give him again to drink, and tell him his name, and promised that he would give him a gift such as a host should give. 2. They told him that if no man does him wrong, they could not help him.

Lesson 21

ℭℛ

from THE ODYSSEY OF HOMER
Translated by Henry Alford

Thence we sailed onward, grieving in our spirits;
And to the shore of the haughty lawless Cyclops
We came, who trusting to the gods immortal
Plant with their hands no plant, nor tillage practise:
But all things grow unsown, and without ploughing,
Barley, and wheat, and vines, which bear abundant no
Wine from their bunches, — all by heaven's rain nourished.
Laws have they none, nor counselling assemblies,
But on the heads of lofty mountains dwell they,
In caverns smooth: each rules unfettered over
His wife and children, and for other cares not.
A fertile island off the harbour stretches
Of the Cyclopian land, not near, nor distant,
Wooded: and in it breed goats without number,
Untamed: for haunts of men are none to fright them,
Nor hunters chase them, who in savage forest
Hardships endure, the tops of hills frequenting.
Nor is it held by tended flocks, nor tillage,
But through all time unsown, unturned by ploughshare,
Of men is void, and bleating flocks supporteth.
For ships vermilion-prowed the Cyclops have not,
Nor men to build them vessels, who might shape out
Well-banked ships, which might their wants supplying
Take them to towns of men; as wander many,
Crossing in ships the seas to one another,
Who this fair island might have wrought with tillage.
Barren it is not, but would all in season
Have borne: and there are meadows by the sea-board
Marshy and rank, where vines might nobly flourish.
Smooth were the soil for ploughs: rich waving wheat-crops
Would wait the harvest: deep and fat the subsoil.
There too is a still harbour, where no need is
Of rope, nor casting anchor, nor of moorings:

But only to put in and wait, till urges
The sailors' spirit, and the breezes whistle.
And at the harbour's head runs limpid water,
A fountain from a cave; and round grow poplars.
There we sailed in, some god our vessels guiding
Through the dark night; nor was the coast apparent:
Dense fog hung round the ships, nor shone upon us
The moon from heaven, for veiling clouds concealed her.

℣

Lesson 21.1

Prose & Poetry

LITERARY ELEMENTS

3 Observe the Invention and Arrangement
+ **Lyrical Elements**

- He describes the land of the Cyclopes, their agriculture and ways of living, along with a nearby island and its wildlife
- Primarily sense of sight
- Ships compared with persons (cheeks of vermilion)

4 Investigate the Context
+ Identify the poem's **Literary Genre**

- **Genre by literary period** – 20th century translation of ancient Greek epic
- **Genre by poetic/narrative category** – a brief lyrical descriptive passage in a poem that is otherwise narrative

SCANSION

The poetic meter is loosely iambic (try some lines in the middle); the lack of rhyming lines make the form blank verse.

Lesson 21.1

Language Logic

SENTENCE DIAGRAMMING AND PARSING

[I stood up (in the ship) and shouted, ["He was no coward, O Cyclops, [whose comrades thou didst so foully slay (in thy den.")]]]

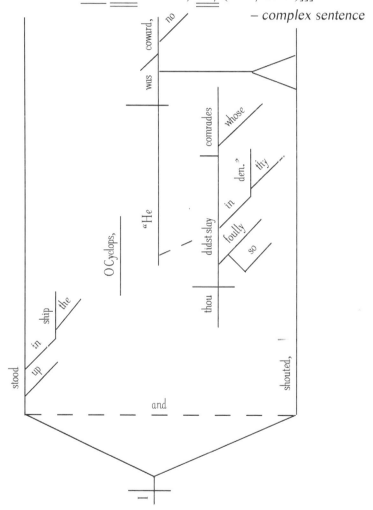

– complex sentence

Nota Bene: *If a relative pronoun has a function in the clause it introduces, it is
diagrammed according to that role. In its subordinate clause,* whose *modifies*
comrades; *it is diagrammed accordingly.*

WORD	PART OF SPEECH	DEFINE	CLASSIFY	PROPERTIES	FUNCTION
was	verb	state/ being	linking	3rd singular past	main verb of principal clause
so	adverb	modifies an adverb	--	--	modifies *foully*
didst slay	verb	action	transitive	3rd singular past	main verb of subordinate clause
den	noun	place	common	3rd singular neuter	OP *in*

Lesson 21.4

Eloquent Expression

LITERARY IMITATION

[A small <u>brook</u> <u><u>glides</u></u> through it, with just murmur enough to lull one to repose;] [and the occasional <u>whistle</u> of a quail or tapping of a woodpecker <u><u>is</u></u> almost the only sound [that ever <u><u>breaks</u></u> in upon the uniform tranqui<u><u>ll</u></u>ity.]]
                                        — *compound-complex sentence*

Figure of description: topographia; Figures of speech: personification — brook glides and murmurs, sound breaks in

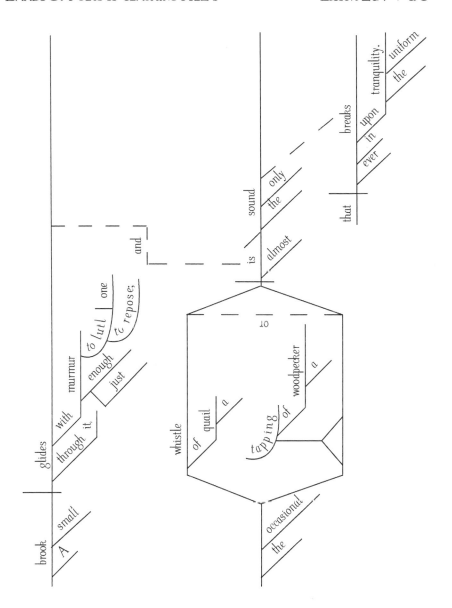

Lesson 22

☙

from THE RAVEN

Once upon a midnight dreary, while I pondered, weak and weary,
Over many a quaint and curious volume of forgotten lore —
While I nodded, nearly napping, suddenly there came a tapping,
As of some one gently rapping, rapping at my chamber door.
"'Tis some visitor," I muttered, "tapping at my chamber door —
    Only this and nothing more."

Ah, distinctly I remember it was in the bleak December;
And each separate dying ember wrought its ghost upon the floor.
Eagerly I wished the morrow; — vainly I had sought to borrow
From my books surcease of sorrow — sorrow for the lost Lenore —
For the rare and radiant maiden whom the angels name Lenore —
    Nameless here for evermore.

And the silken, sad, uncertain rustling of each purple curtain
Thrilled me — filled me with fantastic terrors never felt before;
So that now, to still the beating of my heart, I stood repeating
"'Tis some visitor entreating entrance at my chamber door —
Some late visitor entreating entrance at my chamber door; —
    This it is and nothing more."

 Presently my soul grew stronger; hesitating then no longer,
"Sir," said I, "or Madam, truly your forgiveness I implore;
But the fact is I was napping, and so gently you came rapping,
And so faintly you came tapping, tapping at my chamber door,
That I scarce was sure I heard you" — here I opened wide the door; ——
    Darkness there and nothing more.

Deep into that darkness peering, long I stood there wondering, fearing,
Doubting, dreaming dreams no mortal ever dared to dream before;
But the silence was unbroken, and the stillness gave no token,
And the only word there spoken was the whispered word, "Lenore?"
This I whispered, and an echo murmured back the word, "Lenore!" —

Merely this and nothing more.

Back into the chamber turning, all my soul within me burning,
Soon again I heard a tapping somewhat louder than before.
"Surely," said I, "surely that is something at my window lattice;
Let me see, then, what thereat is, and this mystery explore —
Let my heart be still a moment and this mystery explore;—
    'Tis the wind and nothing more!"

Open here I flung the shutter, when, with many a flirt and flutter,
In there stepped a stately Raven of the saintly days of yore;
Not the least obeisance made he; not a minute stopped or stayed he;
But, with mien of lord or lady, perched above my chamber door —
Perched upon a bust of Pallas just above my chamber door —
    Perched, and sat, and nothing more.

Then this ebony bird beguiling my sad fancy into smiling,
By the grave and stern decorum of the countenance it wore,
"Though thy crest be shorn and shaven, thou," I said, "art sure no craven,
Ghastly grim and ancient Raven wandering from the Nightly shore —
Tell me what thy lordly name is on the Night's Plutonian shore!"
Quoth the Raven "Nevermore."

— EDGAR ALLAN POE

℞

Lesson 22.1

Prose & Poetry

LITERARY ELEMENTS

3 Observe the Invention and Arrangement
  ◆ **Lyrical Elements**
  - Describes the night, the weather, Lenore, the sound of
    tapping, the Raven
  - He describes the sight and sound of things that he describes

to heighten the impression of sadness, melancholy, and
horror.

- He compares shadow of the fire to ghosts, his soul to a fire, the Raven to a lord or lady.

◆ **Narrative Elements**
- **Setting** "a midnight dreary" in "bleak December"
- **Characters** the narrator and a Raven
- **Conflict** In this passage, the poet is pondering "weak and weary," sorrowing for his lost Lenore, and hears a mysterious tapping. (If you read the rest of the poem, you will see the conflict is his wondering about whether he will see her again.)
- **Resolution** Finally, he discovers it is a raven, who enters his study. (In the full poem, the Raven offers no hope, and haunts the poet still.)
- **Sequence** chronological order of events, but he is telling the tale in retrospect.
- **Point of View** 1st person limited

4 **Investigate the Context**
◆ Identify the poem's **Literary Genre**
- **Genre by literary period** – 19th century American
- **Genre by poetic/narrative category** – narrative

Language Logic

SENTENCE DIAGRAMMING AND PARSING
[Open here I flung the shutter,] [when, (with many a flirt and flutter),
In there stepped a stately Raven (of the saintly days) (of yore);]

– complex sentence

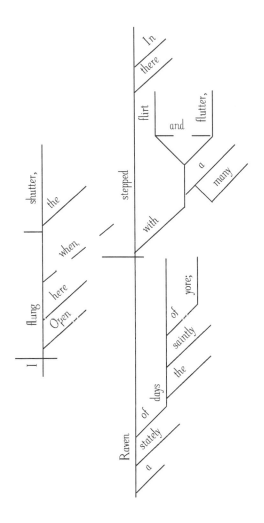

WORD	PART OF SPEECH	DEFINE	CLASSIFY	PROPERTIES	FUNCTION
Open	adverb	modifies a verb	--	--	modifies *flung*
when	conjunction	connects two clauses	subordinate	--	introduces subordinate clause

WORD	PART OF SPEECH	DEFINE	CLASSIFY	PROPERTIES	FUNCTION
there	adverb	modifies a verb	--	--	modifies *stepped*
stepped	verb	action	intransitive	3rd singular past	main verb in subordinate clause
Raven	noun	thing (personified)	proper	3rd singular masculine	subject of subordinate clause
of yore	prepositional phrase	relates *yore* to *days*	--	--	adjectival, modifying *days*

Lesson 22.2

Prose & Poetry

SCANSION AND ANALYSIS

Rhyme Scheme: ABCBBB

Stanza Name: Sextain

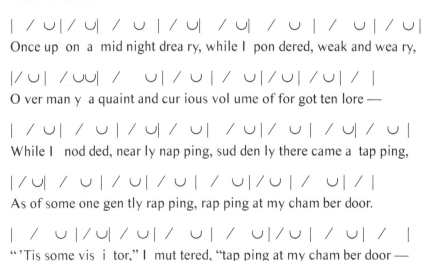

| ∕ ∪| ∕ ∪|∕ ∪ | ∕ |
On ly this and no thing more."

|∕ ∪| ∕ ∪|∕∪| ∕ ∪ |∕ ∪ |∕∪| ∕ ∪| ∕ ∪|
Ah, dis tinc tly I re mem ber it was in the bleak De cem ber;

| ∕ ∪ | ∕ ∪ |∕ ∪|∕∪| ∕ ∪| ∕ ∪|∕ ∪| ∕ |
And each sep arate dy ing em ber wrought its ghost up on the floor.

|∕∪|∕∪| ∕ ∪| ∕ ∪| ∕ ∪|∕ ∪| ∕ ∪| ∕ ∪|
Ea ger ly I wished the mor row; — vain ly I had sought to bor row

| ∕ ∪| ∕ ∪| ∕ ∪|∕ ∪ | ∕ ∪| ∕ ∪|∕ ∪| ∕ |
From my books sur cease of sor row — sor row for the lost Len ore —

| ∕ ∪| ∕ ∪|∕ ∪ | ∕ ∪| ∕ ∪|∕ ∪| ∕ ∪| ∕ |
For the rare and ra diant maid en whom the an gels name Len ore —

| ∕ ∪| ∕ ∪|∕ ∪| ∕ |
Name less here for ev er more.

<hr/>

Lesson 22.3

Prose & Poetry

SCANSION

Note that the second line of the stanza below (the fourth stanza of the poem) has only seven feet.

| ∕ ∪|∕∪| ∕ ∪ | ∕ ∪| ∕∪|∕ ∪| ∕ ∪| ∕ ∪|
Pres ent ly my soul grew strong er; hes i ta ting then no long er,

| ∕ ∪|∕∪| ∕ ∪ | ∕∪| ∕ ∪| ∕ ∪|∕ ∪ ∪|
"Sir," said I, "or Mad am, tru ly your for give ness I im plore;

| ∕∪| ∕ ∪|∕ ∪| ∕ ∪ | ∕∪| ∕ ∪|∕ ∪| ∕ ∪|
But the fact is I was nap ping, and so gen tly you came rap ping,

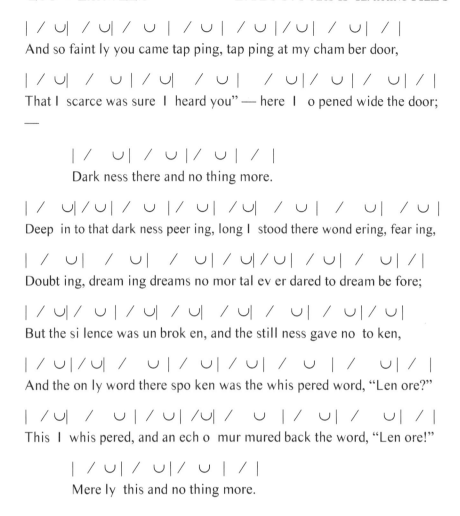

| / ∪| / ∪| / ∪ | / ∪ | / ∪ |/ ∪| / ∪| / |
And so faint ly you came tap ping, tap ping at my cham ber door,

| / ∪| / ∪ | / ∪| / ∪ | / ∪|/ ∪ | / ∪| / |
That I scarce was sure I heard you" — here I o pened wide the door;

—

| / ∪| / ∪ |/ ∪ | / |
Dark ness there and no thing more.

| / ∪|/∪| / ∪ |/ ∪| /∪| / ∪ | / ∪| / ∪|
Deep in to that dark ness peer ing, long I stood there wond ering, fear ing,

| / ∪| / ∪| / ∪| / ∪|/∪| / ∪| / ∪| /|
Doubt ing, dream ing dreams no mor tal ev er dared to dream be fore;

| / ∪|/ ∪ | / ∪| / ∪| / ∪| / ∪| / ∪|/ ∪|
But the si lence was un brok en, and the still ness gave no to ken,

| / ∪|/∪| / ∪| / ∪|/∪| / ∪ | / ∪| / |
And the on ly word there spo ken was the whis pered word, "Len ore?"

| /∪| / ∪| / ∪| /∪| / ∪ | / ∪| / ∪| / |
This I whis pered, and an ech o mur mured back the word, "Len ore!"

| / ∪| / ∪|/ ∪ | / |
Mere ly this and no thing more.

Eloquent Expression

FIGURES OF SPEECH – ALLITERATION AND ONOMATOPOEIA

Representative, not exhaustive.

Alliteration in "The Raven": (there may be more; these are the most obvious): weak and weary; quaint and curious (k sound); nodded, nearly napping; surcease of sorrow; rare and radiant; silken, sad un-certain; filled

me with fantastic terrors never felt before; entreating entrance; soul grew
stronger; scarce was sure; Deep into that darkness...Doubting, dreaming dreams no mortal dared to dream before; word there spoken was the
whispered word; surely that is something; flirt and flutter; stepped a stately Raven of the saintly days; obeisance made he, not a minute stopped
or stayed he; Perched upon a bust of Pallas; this ebony bird beguiling my
sad fancy into smiling; shorn and shaven; ghastly grim.

Onomatopoeia in "The Raven": (there may be more; these are the most
obvious): tapping, rapping, rustling, beating, whispered, murmured, flutter

Anastrophe in "The Raven" (a few examples): I scarce was sure I
heard you, Deep into that darkness peering, long I stood there, Back
into the chamber turning, In there stepped a stately Raven, Not the least
obeisance made he, Quoth the raven, "Nevermore."

Simile in "The Raven": none

Metaphor in "The Raven": (there may be more; these are the most
obvious) silence was unbroken; Night's Plutonian shore

Personification in "The Raven": dying ember wrought its ghost; sad,
uncertain rustling of each purple curtain; soul grew stronger; stillness gave
no token; heart be still...explore; stately Raven; saintly days of yore; grave
and stern decorum of the countenance it wore; thy lordly name is

A few examples of alliteration in other poems we have studied
(there are many more!): "The Reading Mother" Sagas of pirate who
scoured the sea; "The Destruction of Sennacherib" Their hearts but
once heaved; "The Land of Story-Books" At evening when the lamp is
lit; "A Book" This traverse may the poorest take without oppress of Toll;
"A Visit from St. Nicholas" Away to the window I flew like a flash

A few examples of onomatopoeia in other poems we have studied

(there are many more!): "The Destruction of Sennacherib" gasping,
wail; "Hiawatha" whispering, Minne-wawa; "A Visit from St. Nicholas"
clatter, whistled

Lesson 22.4

Prose & Poetry

SCANSION:

|/ ∪| / ∪| / ∪| / ∪| /　　∪| /∪∪| / ∪| /∪|
O pen here I flung the shut ter, when, with man y a flirt and flut ter,

|/ ∪ | / ∪| / ∪| / ∪|/ ∪| / ∪| / ∪| / |
In there stepped a state ly Ra ven of the saint ly days of yore;

| / ∪| / ∪|/ ∪ | / ∪| /∪| / ∪| / ∪| / ∪ |
Not the least o bei sance made he; not a min ute stopped or stayed he;

| / ∪ | / ∪| / ∪|/ ∪| / ∪| / ∪| / ∪| / |
But, with mien of lord or la dy, perched a bove my cham ber door —

| / ∪| / ∪| / ∪| / ∪| /∪| / ∪| / ∪| / |
Perched up on a bust of Pal las just a bove my cham ber door —

| / ∪| / ∪|/ ∪ | / |
Perched, and sat, and no thing more.

| / ∪|/ ∪∪| / ∪| / ∪| / ∪| /∪|/ ∪| / ∪ |
Then this e bon y bird be guil ing my sad fan cy in to smil ing,

|/ ∪| / ∪| / ∪|/ ∪|/ ∪| / ∪| / ∪| / |
By the grave and stern de cor um of the coun ten ance it wore,

| / ∪| / ∪| / ∪| / ∪| / ∪| / ∪| / ∪|/ ∪|
"Though thy crest be shorn and shav en, thou," I said, "art sure no cra ven,

| / ∪| / ∪|/ ∪|/ ∪| / ∪ | / ∪| / ∪| / |

Ghast ly grim and an cient Ra ven wan dering from the Night ly shore —

| / ∪| / ∪| / ∪| / ∪| / ∪ | / ∪| / ∪| / |

Tell me what thy lord ly name is on the Night's Plut o nian shore!"

| / ∪| / ∪| / ∪| / |

Quoth the Ra ven "Nev er more."

Lesson 22.5

Language Logic

SENTENCE DIAGRAMMING AND PARSING

[Not the least obeisance made he;] [not a minute stopped or stayed he;]
[But, with mien of lord or lady, perched above my chamber door.]

– compound sentence

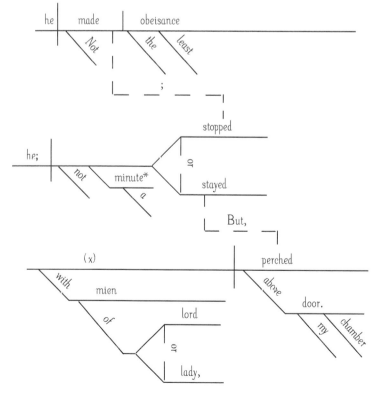

Minute is an adverbial noun here. See Sentence Sense – Modifiers: Adverbial Nouns

Nota Bene: Diagramming is an art! We have diagrammed the prepositional phrase *with mien of lord or lady* as an adjective element modifying *he*. It could also be construed as an adverb element modifying *perched*. The diagram decision here will depend on whether one thinks of the Raven's mien being inherent to the Raven himself, or whether one considers it the manner with which he perched himself above the door. In light of the poetic context, the first seems slightly preferable, but the second is also completely plausible. We would absolutely require the students to defend their choice, and even bring this possibility up in class as a thinking exercise even if no one diagrams it as an adverb element. This is a marvlous opporunity to illustrate to students the combination of logic, ordered thinking, analysis, and interpretation is required by the valuable practice of sentence diagramming. It is also a great reminder for us as teachers as to why we want to continue this important pedagogical tool.

WORD	PART OF SPEECH	DEFINE	CLASSIFY	PROPERTIES	FUNCTION
Not	adverb	modifies a verb	--	--	modifies *made*
obeisance	noun	idea	common	3rd singular neuter	DO *made*
he	pronoun	stands in for *Raven*	personal	3rd singular masculine	Subject of main clause (either first or second)
stopped	verb	action	instransitive	3rd singular past	main verb of principal clause
above my chamber door	prepositional phrase	relates *door* to *perched*	--	--	adverbial, modifies *perched*

Lesson 23

♋

KING ARTHUR

from HEROES EVERY CHILD SHOULD KNOW **by Hamilton Wright Mabie**

[Prologue] Long years ago, there ruled over Britain a King called Uther Pendragon. A mighty prince was he, and feared by all men; yet, when he sought the love of the fair Igraine of Cornwall, she would have naught to do with him, so that, from grief and disappointment, Uther fell sick, and at last seemed like to die.

Now in those days, there lived a famous magician named Merlin, so powerful that he could change his form at will, or even make himself invisible; nor was there any place so remote but that he could reach it at once, merely by wishing himself there. [Action 1] One day, suddenly he stood at Uther's bedside, and said: "Sir King, I know thy grief, and am ready to help thee. Only promise to give me, at his birth, the son that shall be born to thee, and thou shalt have thy heart's desire." To this the King agreed joyfully, and Merlin kept his word: for he gave Uther the form of one whom Igraine had loved dearly, and so she took him willingly for her husband.

[Action 2 – Physical, Time] When the time had come that a child should be born to the King and Queen, Merlin appeared before Uther to remind him of his promise; and Uther swore it should be as he had said. Three days later, a prince was born and, with pomp and ceremony, was christened by the name of Arthur; but immediately thereafter, the King commanded that the child should be carried to the postern-gate, there to be given to the old man who would be found waiting without.

[Action 3 – Physical, Time] Not long after, Uther fell sick, and he knew that his end was come; so, by Merlin's advice; he called together his knights and barons, and said to them: "My death draws near. I charge you, therefore, that ye obey my son even as ye have obeyed me; and my curse upon him if he claim not the crown when he is a man grown." Then the King turned his face to the wall and died.

[Action 4 − Time, Action, Person] Scarcely was Uther laid in his grave before disputes arose. Few of the nobles had seen Arthur or even heard of him, and not one of them would have been willing to be ruled by a child; rather, each thought himself fitted to be King, and, strengthening his own castle, made war on his neighbours until confusion alone was supreme and the poor groaned because there was none to help them.

[Action 5 − Person, Action] Now when Merlin carried away Arthur—for Merlin was the old man who had stood at the postern-gate—he had known all that would happen, and had taken the child to keep him safe from the fierce barons until he should be of age to rule wisely and well, and perform all the wonders prophesied of him. He gave the child to the care of the good knight Sir Ector to bring up with his son Kay, but revealed not to him that it was the son of Uther Pendragon that was given into his charge.

[Action 6 − Time, Action, Place] At last, when years had passed and Arthur was grown a tall youth well skilled in knightly exercises, Merlin went to the Archbishop of Canterbury and advised him that he should call together at Christmas-time all the chief men of the realm to the great cathedral in London; "For," said Merlin, "there shall be seen a great marvel by which it shall be made clear to all men who is the lawful King of this land." The Archbishop did as Merlin counselled. Under pain of a fearful curse, he bade barons and knights come to London to keep the feast, and to pray heaven to send peace to the realm.

[Action 7 − Physical] The people hastened to obey the Arch-bishop's commands, and, from all sides, barons and knights came riding in to keep the birth-feast of our Lord. And when they had prayed, and were coming forth from the cathedral, they saw a strange sight. There, in the open space before the church, stood, on a great stone, an anvil thrust through with a sword; and on the stone were written these words: "Whoso can draw forth this sword, is rightful King of Britain born."

At once there were fierce quarrels, each man clamouring to be the first to try his fortune, none doubting his own success. Then the Archbishop decreed that each should make the venture in turn, from the greatest baron to the least knight, and each in turn, having put forth his utmost strength, failed to move the sword one inch, and drew back ashamed. So the Archbishop dismissed the company, and having appointed guards to watch over the stone, sent messengers through all the land to give word of great jousts to be held in London at Easter, when each knight could give proof of his skill and courage, and try whether the adventure of the sword was for him.

[Action 8 – Person, Action] Among those who rode to London at Easter was the good Sir Ector, and with him his son, Sir Kay, newly made a knight, and the young Arthur. When the morning came that the jousts should begin, Sir Kay and Arthur mounted their horses and set out for the lists; but before they reached the field, Kay looked and saw that he had left his sword behind. Immediately Arthur turned back to fetch it for him, only to find the house fast shut, for all were gone to view the tournament. Sore vexed was Arthur, fearing lest his brother Kay should lose his chance of gaining glory, till, of a sudden, he bethought him of the sword in the great anvil before the cathedral. Thither he rode with all speed, and the guards having deserted their post to view the tournament, there was none to forbid him the adventure. He leapt from his horse, seized the hilt, and instantly drew forth the sword as easily as from a scabbard; then, mounting his horse and thinking no marvel of what he had done, he rode after his brother and handed him the weapon.

[Action 9 – Person] When Kay looked at it, he saw at once that it was the wondrous sword from the stone. In great joy he sought his father, and showing it to him, said: "Then must I be King of Britain." But Sir Ector bade him say how he came by the sword, and when Sir Kay told how Arthur had brought it to him, Sir Ector bent his knee to the boy, and said: "Sir, I perceive that ye are my King, and here I tender you my homage"; and Kay did as his father. [Action 10 – Person, Place] Then the three sought the Archbishop, to whom they related all that had happened; and he, much marvelling, called the people together to the great stone, and bade Arthur thrust back the sword and draw it forth again in the presence of all, which he did with ease. But an angry murmur arose from the barons, who cried that what a boy could do, a man could do; so, at the Archbishop's word, the sword was put back, and each man, whether baron or knight, tried in his turn to draw it forth, and failed. Then, for the third time, Arthur drew forth the sword. Immediately there arose from the people a great shout: "Arthur is King! Arthur is King! We will have no King but Arthur"; and, though the great barons scowled and threatened, they fell on their knees before him while the Archbishop placed the crown upon his head, and swore to obey him faithfully as their lord and sovereign.

[Summary] Thus Arthur was made King; and to all he did justice, righting wrongs and giving to all their dues. Nor was he forgetful of those that had been his friends; for Kay, whom he loved as a brother, he made Seneschal and chief of his household, and to Sir Ector, his foster father, he gave broad lands.

[Action 10 – Person, Action, Time] Thus Arthur was made King, but he had to fight for his own; for eleven great kings drew together and refused to acknowledge him as their lord, and chief amongst the rebels was King Lot of Orknev who had married Arthur's sister, Bellicent.

By Merlin's advice, Arthur sent for help overseas, to Ban and Bors, the two great Kings who ruled in Gaul. With their aid, he overthrew shis foes in a great battle near the river Trent; and then he passed with them into their own lands and helped them drive out their enemies. So there was ever great friendship between Arthur and the Kings Ban and Bors, and all their kindred; and afterward some of the most famous Knights of the Round Table were of that kin.

[Summary/Explanation] Then King Arthur set himself to restore order throughout his kingdom. To all who would submit and amend their evil ways, he showed kindness; but those who persisted in oppression and wrong he removed, putting in their places others who would deal justly with the people. And because the land had become overrun with forest during the days of misrule, he cut roads through the thickets, that no longer wild beasts and men, fiercer than the beasts, should lurk in their gloom, to the harm of the weak and defenceless. Thus it came to pass that soon the peasant ploughed his fields in safety, and where had been wastes, men dwelt again in peace and prosperity.

[Action 11 – Person, Action] Amongst the lesser Kings whom Arthur helped to rebuild their towns and restore order, was King Leodegrance of Cameliard. Now Leodegrance had one fair child, his daughter Guenevere; and from the time that first he saw her, Arthur gave her all his love. So he sought counsel of Merlin, his chief adviser. Merlin heard the King sorrowfully, and he said: "Sir King, when a man's heart is set, he may not change. Yet had it been well if ye had loved another."

So the King sent his knights to Leodegrance, to ask of him his daughter; and Leodegrance consented, rejoicing to wed her to so good and knightly a King. With great pomp, the princess was conducted to Canterbury, and there the King met her, and they two were wed by the Archbishop in the great Cathedral, amid the rejoicings of the people.

[Action 12 – Physical, Person] On that same day did Arthur found his Order of the Round Table, the fame of which was to spread throughout Christendom and endure through all time. Now the Round Table had been made for King Uther Pendragon by Merlin, who had meant thereby to set forth plainly to all men the roundness of the earth. After Uther died, King Leodegrance had possessed it; but when Arthur was wed, he sent it to him as a gift, and great was the King's joy at receiving it. One hundred and fifty knights might take their places about it, and for them Merlin made sieges, or seats. One hundred and twenty-eight did Arthur knight at that great feast; thereafter, if any sieges were empty, at the high festival of Pentecost new knights were ordained to fill them, and by magic was the name of each knight found inscribed, in letters of gold, in his proper siege. One seat only long remained unoccupied, and that was the Siege Perilous. No knight might occupy it until the coming of Sir Galahad; for, without danger to his life, none might sit there who was not free from all stain of sin.

With pomp and ceremony did each knight take upon him the vows of true knighthood: to obey the King; to show mercy to all who asked it; to defend the weak; and for no worldly gain to fight in a wrongful cause: and all the knights rejoiced together, doing honour to Arthur and to his Queen. Then they rode forth to right the wrong and help the oppressed, and by their aid the King held his realm in peace, doing justice to all.

[Transition] Now, as time passed, King Arthur gathered into his Order of the Round Table knights whose peers shall never be found in any age; and foremost amongst them all was Sir Launcelot du Lac. Such was his strength that none against whom he laid lance in rest could keep the saddle, and no shield was proof against his sword dint; but for his courtesy even more than for his courage and strength, Sir Launcelot was famed far and near. Gentle he was and ever the first to rejoice in the renown of another; and in the jousts, he would avoid encounter with the young and untried knight, letting him pass to gain glory if he might.

[Explanation] It would take a great book to record all the famous deeds of Sir Launcelot, and all his adventures. He was of Gaul, for his father, King Ban, ruled over Benwick; he was named Launcelot du Lac by the Lady of the Lake who reared him when his mother died. Early he won renown; then, when there was peace in his own land, he passed into Britain, to Arthur's Court, where the King received him gladly, and made him Knight of the Round Table and took him for his trustiest friend. And so it was that, when Guenevere was to be brought to Canterbury, to be married to the King, Launcelot was chief of the knights sent to wait upon her, and of this came the sorrow of later days. For, from the moment he saw her, Sir Launcelot loved Guenevere, for her sake remaining wifeless all his days, and in all things being her faithful knight. But busy-bodies and mischief – makers spoke evil of Sir Launcelot and the Queen, and from their talk came the undoing of the King and the downfall of his great work. But that was after long years, and after many true knights had lived their lives, honouring the King and Queen, and doing great deeds.

[Action 13 – Person] Before Merlin passed from the world of men, he had uttered many marvellous prophesies, and one that boded ill to King Arthur; for he foretold that, in the days to come, a son of Arthur's sister should stir up bitter war against the King, and at last a great battle should be fought, when many a brave knight should find his doom.

[Action 14 – Person] Now, among the nephews of Arthur, was one most dishonourable; his name was Mordred. No knightly deed had he ever done, and he hated to hear the good report of others because he himself was a coward and envious. But of all the Round Table there was none that Mordred hated more than Sir Launcelot du Lac, whom all true knights held in most honour; and not the less did Mordred hate Launcelot that he was the knight whom Queen

Guenevere had in most esteem. So, at last, his jealous rage passing all bounds, he spoke evil of the Queen and of Launcelot, saying that they were traitors to the King. Now Sir Gawain and Sir Gareth, Mordred's brothers, refused to give ear to these slanders, holding that Sir Launcelot, in his knightly service of the Queen, did honour to King Arthur also; but by ill-fortune another brother, Sir Agravaine, had ill-will to the Queen, and professed to believe Mordred's evil tales. So the two went to King Arthur with their ill stories.

Now when Arthur had heard them, he was wroth; for never would he lightly believe evil of any, and Sir Launcelot was the knight whom he loved above all others. Sternly then he bade them begone and come no more to him with unproven tales against any, and, least of all, against Sir Launcelot and their lady, the Queen.

The two departed, but in their hearts was hatred against Launcelot and the Queen, more bitter than ever for the rebuke they had called down upon themselves.

[Action 15 — Person, Action] Great was the King's grief. Despite all that Mordred could say, he was slow to doubt Sir Launcelot, whom he loved, but his mind was filled with forebodings; and well he knew that their kin would seek vengeance on Sir Launcelot, and the noble fellowship of the Round Table be utterly destroyed.

All too soon it proved even as the King had feared. Many were found to hold with Sir Mordred; some from envy of the honour and worship of the noble Sir Launcelot; and among them even were those who dared to raise their voice against the Queen herself, calling for judgment upon her as leagued with a traitor against the King, and as having caused the death of so many good knights. Now in those days the law was that if any one were accused of treason by witnesses, or taken in the act, that one should die the death by burning, be it man or woman, knight or churl. So then the murmurs grew to a loud clamour that the law should have its course, and that King Arthur should pass sentence on the Queen. Then was the King's woe doubled; "For," said he, "I sit as King to be a rightful judge and keep all the law; wherefore I may not do battle for my own Queen, and now there is none other to help her." So a decree was issued that Queen Guenevere should be burnt at the stake outside the walls of Carlisle.

[Action 16 — Person, Action] Forthwith, King Arthur sent

for his nephew, Sir Gawain, and said to him: "Fair nephew, I give it
in charge to you to see that all is done as has been decreed." But Sir
Gawain answered boldly: "Sir King, never will I be present to see
my lady the Queen die. It is of ill counsel that ye have consented to
her death." Then the King bade Gawain send his two young brothers, Sir Gareth and Sir Gaheris, to receive his commands, and these
he desired to attend the Queen to the place of execution. So Gareth
made answer for both: "My Lord the King, we owe you obedience in
all things, but know that it is sore against our wills that we obey you
in this; nor will we appear in arms in the place where that noble lady
shall die"; then sorrowfully they mounted their horses and rode to
Carlisle.

[Action 17 − Time] When the day appointed had come, the
Queen was led forth to a place without the walls of Carlisle, and
there she was bound to the stake to be burnt to death. Loud were
her ladies' lamentations, and many a lord was found to weep at that
grievous sight of a Queen brought so low; yet was there none who
dared come forward as her champion, lest he should be suspected of
treason. As for Gareth and Gaheris, they could not bear the sight and
stood with their faces covered in their mantles. [Action 18 − Physical, person] Then, just as the torch was to be applied to the faggots,
there was a sound as of many horses galloping, and the next instant a
band of knights rushed upon the astonished throng, their leader cutting down all who crossed his path until he had reached the Queen,
whom he lifted to his saddle and bore from the press. Then all men
knew that it was Sir Launcelot, come knightly to rescue the Queen,
and in their hearts they rejoiced. So with little hindrance they rode
away, Sir Launcelot and all his kin with the Queen in their midst,
till they came to the castle of the Joyous Garde where they held the
Queen in safety and all reverence.

At last Sir Launcelot desired of King Arthur assurance of liberty
for the Queen, as also safe conduct for himself and his knights, that
he might bring Dame Guenevere, with due honour, to the King at
Carlisle; and thereto the King pledged his word.

[Action 19 − Physical, Place] So Launcelot set forth with the
Queen, and behind them rode a hundred knights arrayed in green
velvet, the housings of the horses of the same all studded with precious stones; thus they passed through the city of Carlisle, openly,

in the sight of all, and there were many who rejoiced that the Queen was come again and Sir Launcelot with her, though they of Gawain's party scowled upon him.

When they were come into the great hall where Arthur sat, with Sir Gawain and other great lords about him, Sir Launcelot led Guenevere to the throne and both knelt before the King; then, rising, Sir Launcelot lifted the Queen to her feet, and thus he spoke to King Arthur, boldly and well before the whole court: "My lord, Sir Arthur, I bring you here your Queen, than whom no truer nor nobler lady ever lived; and here stand I, Sir Launcelot du Lac, ready to do battle with any that dare gainsay it"; and with these words Sir Launcelot turned and looked upon the lords and knights present in their places, but none would challenge him in that cause, not even Sir Gawain, for he had ever affirmed that Dame Guenevere was a true and honourable lady.

Then Sir Launcelot spoke again; "Now, my Lord Arthur, in my own defence it behooves me to say that never in aught have I been false to you."

"Peace," said the King to Sir Launcelot: "We give you fifteen days in which to leave this kingdom." Then Sir Launcelot sighed heavily and said: "Full well I see that nothing availeth me." Then he went to the Queen where she sat, and said: "Madam, the time is come when I must leave this fair realm that I have loved. Think well of me, I pray you, and send for me if ever there be aught in which a true knight may serve lady." Therewith he turned him about and, without greeting to any, passed through the hall, and with his faithful knights rode to the Joyous Garde, though ever thereafter, in memory of that sad day, he called it the Dolorous Garde.

[Action 20 – Time, Place] In after times when the King had passed overseas to France, leaving Sir Mordred to rule Britain in his stead, there came messengers from Britain bearing letters for King Arthur; and more evil news than they brought might not well be, for they told how Sir Mordred had usurped his uncle's realm. First, he had caused it to be noised abroad that King Arthur was slain in battle with Sir Launcelot, and, since there be many ever ready to believe any idle rumour and eager for any change, it had been no hard task for Sir Mordred to call the lords to a Parliament and persuade them to make him King. But the Queen could not be brought to believe that her lord was dead, so she took refuge in the Tower of London from Sir Mordred's violence, nor was she to be induced to leave her strong refuge for aught that Mordred could promise or threaten.

[Action 21 – Place] Forthwith, King Arthur bade his host make ready to move, and when they had reached the coast, they embarked and made sail to reach Britain with all possible speed.

Sir Mordred, on his part, had heard of their sailing, and hasted to get together a great army. It was grievous to see how many a stout knight held by Mordred, ay, even many whom Arthur himself had raised to honour and fortune; for it is the nature of men to be fickle. Thus is was that, when Arthur drew near to Dover, he found Mordred with a mighty host, waiting to oppose his landing. Then there was a great sea-fight, those of Mordred's party going out in boats, to board King Arthur's ships and slay him and his men or ever they should come to land. Right valiantly did King Arthur bear him, as was his wont, and boldly his followers fought in his cause, so that at last they drove off their enemies and landed at Dover in spite of Mordred and his array.

Now, by this time, many that Mordred had cheated by his lying reports, had drawn unto King Arthur, to whom at heart they had ever been loyal, knowing him for a true and noble King and hating themselves for having been deceived by such a false usurper as Sir Mordred.

[Action 22 – Time] One night, as King Arthur slept, he thought that Sir Gawain stood before him, looking just as he did in life, and said to him: "My uncle and my King, God in his great love has suffered me to come unto you, to warn you that in no wise ye fight on the morrow; for if ye do, ye shall be slain, and with you the most part of the people on both sides. Make ye, therefore, a treaty." Immediately, the King awoke and called to him the best and wisest of his knights. Then all were agreed that, on any terms whatsoever, a treaty should be made with Sir Mordred, even as Sir Gawain had said; and, with the dawn, messengers went to the camp of the enemy, to call Sir Mordred to a conference. So it was determined that the meeting should take place in the sight of both armies, in an open space between the two camps, and that King Arthur and Mordred should each be accompanied by fourteen knights. Little enough faith had either in the other, so when they set forth to the meeting, they bade their hosts join battle if ever they saw a sword drawn.

Now as they talked, it befell that an adder, coming out of a bush hard by, stung a knight in the foot; and he, seeing the snake, drew his sword to kill it and thought no harm thereby. [Action 23 — Physical] But on the instant that the sword flashed, the trumpets blared on both sides and the two hosts rushed to battle. Never was there fought a fight of such enmity; for brother fought with brother, and comrade with comrade, and fiercely they cut and thrust, with many a bitter word between; while King Arthur himself, his heart hot within him, rode through and through the battle, seeking the traitor Mordred. So they fought all day, till at last the evening fell. Then Arthur, looking round him, saw of his valiant knights but two left, Sir Lucan and Sir Bedivere, and these sore wounded; and there, over against him, by a great heap of the dead, stood Sir Mordred, the cause of all this ruin. Thereupon the King, his heart nigh broken with grief for the loss of his true knights, cried with a loud voice, "Traitor! now is thy doom upon thee!" and with his spear gripped in both hands, he rushed upon Sir Mordred and smote him that the weapon stood out a fathom behind. And Sir Mordred knew that he had his death wound. With all the might that he had, he thrust him up the spear to the haft and, with his sword, struck King Arthur upon the head, that the steel pierced the helmet and bit into the head; then Mordred fell back, stark and dead.

[Action 24 — Physical, Person] Sir Lucan and Sir Bedivere went to the King where he lay, swooning from the blow, and bore him to a little chapel on the seashore. As they laid him on the ground, Sir Lucan fell dead beside the King, and Arthur, coming to himself, found but Sir Bedivere alive beside him.

So King Arthur lay wounded to the death, grieving, not that his end was come, but for the desolation of his kingdom and the loss of his good knights. And looking upon the body of Sir Lucan, he sighed and said: "Alas! true knight, dead for my sake! If I lived, I should ever grieve for thy death, but now mine own end draws nigh." Then, turning to Sir Bedivere, who stood sorrowing beside him, he said: "Leave weeping now, for the time is short and much to do. Hereafter shalt thou weep if thou wilt. But take now my sword Excalibur, hasten to the water side, and fling it into the deep. Then, watch what happens and bring me word thereof." "My Lord," said Sir Bedivere, "your

command shall be obeyed"; and, taking the sword, he departed.
[Action 25 – Place, Action] But as he went on his way, he looked
on the sword, how wondrously it was formed and the hilt all studded
with precious stones; and, as he looked, he called to mind the marvel
by which it had come into the King's keeping. For on a certain day, as
Arthur walked on the shore of a great lake, there had appeared above
the surface of the water a hand brandishing a sword. On the instant,
the King had leaped into a boat, and, rowing into the lake, had got
the sword and brought it back to land. Then he had seen how, on
one side the blade, was written, "Keep me," but on the other, "Throw
me away," and, sore perplexed, he had shown it to Merlin, the great
wizard, who said: "Keep it now. The time for casting away has not
yet come." Thinking on this, it seemed to Bedivere that no good, but
harm, must come of obeying the King's word; so hiding the sword
under a tree, [Action 26 – place, action] he hastened back to the
little chapel. Then said the King: "What saw'st thou?" "Sir," answered
Bedivere, "I saw naught but the waves, heard naught but the wind."
"That is untrue," said King Arthur; "I charge thee, as thou art true
knight, go again and spare not to throw away the sword."

[Action 27 – Place, Action] Sir Bedivere departed a second
time, and his mind was to obey his lord; but when he took the sword
in his hand, he thought: "Sin it is and shameful, to throw away so
glorious a sword" Then, hiding it again, he hastened back to the
King. [Action 28 – Place, Action] "What saw'st thou?" said Sir
Arthur. "Sir, I saw the water lap on the crags." Then spoke the King in
great wrath: "Traitor and unkind! Twice hast thou betrayed me! Art
dazzled by the splendour of the jewels, thou that, till now, hast ever
been dear and true to me? Go yet again, but if thou fail me this time,
I will arise and, with mine own hands, slay thee."

[Action 29 – Place, Action] Then Sir Bedivere left the King
and, that time, he took the sword quickly from the place where he
had hidden it and, forbearing even to look upon it, he twisted the
belt about it and flung it with all his force into the water. A wondrous
sight he saw for, as the sword touched the water, a hand rose from
out the deep, caught it, brandished it thrice, and drew it beneath the
surface.

[Action 30 – Place, Action] Sir Bedivere hastened back to the
King and told him what he had seen. "It is well," said Arthur; "now,

bear me to the water's edge; and hasten, I pray thee, for I have tarried overlong and my wound has taken cold." So Sir Bedivere raised the King on his back and bore him tenderly to the lonely shore, where the lapping waves floated many an empty helmet and the fitful moonlight fell on the upturned faces of the dead. [Action 33 – Physical, Place, Person] Scarce had they reached the shore when there hove in sight a barge, and on its deck stood three tall women, robed all in black and wearing crowns on their heads. "Place me in the barge," said the King, and softly Sir Bedivere lifted the King into it. And these three Queens wept sore over Arthur, and one took his head in her lap and chafed his hands, crying: "Alas! my brother, thou hast been overlong in coming and, I fear me, thy wound has taken cold." Then the barge began to move slowly from the land. When Sir Bedivere saw this, he lifted up his voice and cried with a bitter cry: "Ah! my Lord Arthur, thou art taken from me! And I, whither shall I go?" "Comfort thyself," said the King, "for in me is no comfort more. I pass to the Valley of Avilion, to heal me of my grievous wound. If thou seest me never again, pray for me."

[Action 31 – [Place, Action] So the barge floated away out of sight, and Sir Bedivere stood straining his eyes after it till it had vanished utterly. Then he turned him about and journeyed through the forest until, at daybreak, he reached a hermitage. Entering it, he prayed the holy hermit that he might abide with him, and there he spent the rest of his life in prayer and holy exercise.

[Summary] But of King Arthur is no more known. Some men, indeed, say that he is not dead, but abides in the happy Valley of Avilion until such time as his country's need is sorest, when he shall come again and deliver it. Others say that, of a truth, he is dead, and that, in the far West, his tomb may be seen, and written on it these words:

> "Here lies Arthur, once King and King to be"

☙

Lesson 23.1

Prose & Poetry

LITERARY ELEMENTS

3 Observe the Invention and Arrangement
- **Lyrical Elements**
  - Describes
  - Senses
  - Comparisons

- **Narrative Elements**
  - **Setting** Early Britain, circa 5th-6th century A.D.
  - **Characters** Uther Pendragon, Merlin, Arthur, Kay, Ector, Guenevere, Sir Launcelot, Galahad, Knights of the Round Table, Mordred, Gawain, Bedivere
  - **Sequence** *ab ovo,* linear (from birth to death of King Arthur)
  - **Point of View** Third person omniscient

4 Investigate the Context
- Identify the poem's **Literary Genre**
  - **Genre by literary period** – early 20th century American retelling of a tale from ancient Britain
  - **Genre by poetic/narrative category** – Treat as non-fiction, with possible fictional details. See discussion in Teaching Helps, Lesson 7.1

5 Connect the Thoughts
- other stories of King Arthur and the Knights of the Round Table – there are many! Note that the story of Guenevere and Launcelot

is different than other versions, many of which allege their guilt,
but her eventual (but too late) repentance

Lesson 23.2

Prose & Poetry

NARRATIVE PLOT ANALYSIS
See suggested scene divisions in selection at beginning of this lesson.
Remember that answers may vary.

Eloquent Expression

COPIA OF CONSTRUCTION: POLYSYNDETON
Answers will vary: 1. The Archbishop dismissed the company, and
appointed guards, and sent messages through all the land. 2. Each knight
did take upon himself the vows of true knighthood: to obey the King, and
to show mercy to all who asked it, and to defend the weak, and to refrain
from fighting for a wrongful cause. 3. He prophesied that bitter war would
be stirred up against the king and a great battle would be fought and many
a brave knight should find his doom.

Lesson 23.3

Language Logic

SENTENCE DIAGRAMMING AND PARSING
[No knight might occupy that seat (until the coming) (of Sir Galahad)];
[for, (without danger) (to his life), none might sit there [who was not free
(from all stain) (of sin).]]   — *compound-complex sentence*

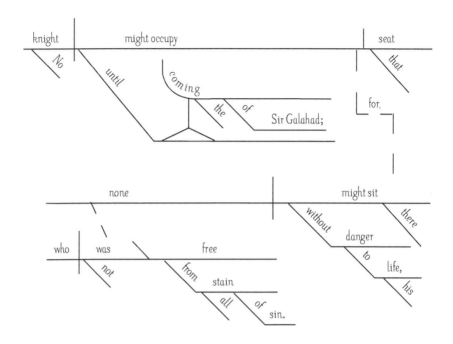

WORD	PART OF SPEECH	DEFINE	CLASSIFY	PROPERTIES	FUNCTION
that	adjective	modifies a noun	definitive	--	modifies *seat*
Sir Galahad	noun	person	proper	3rd singular masculine	OP *of*
to his life	prepositional phrase	relates *life* to *danger*	--	--	adjectival, modifies *danger*
was	verb	state/being	linking	3rd singular past	main verb of relative (subordinate) clause

WORD	PART OF SPEECH	DEFINE	CLASSIFY	PROPERTIES	FUNCTION
there	adverb	modifes a verb	--	--	modifies *sit*

Eloquent Expression

COPIA OF CONSTRUCTION: ASYNDETON

Answers will vary: 1. The Archbishop dismissed the company, appointed guards, sent messages through all the land. 2. Each knight did take upon himself the vows of true knighthood: to obey the King, to show mercy to all who asked it, to defend the weak, to refrain from fighting for a wrongful cause. 3. He prophesied that bitter war would be stirred up against the king, a great battle would be fought, many a brave knight should find his doom.

Lesson 23.5

Eloquent Expression

LITERARY IMITATION

For [many a petty king [ere Arthur came]
Ruled in this isle, and ever waging war
Each (upon other), wasted all the land;]
And [still from time to time the heathen host
Swarmed overseas, and harried [what was left.]]

         – compound-complex sentence

Figure of description: none; Figures of speech: metaphor – heathen host swarmed (compared to insects); anastropher – Each upon other

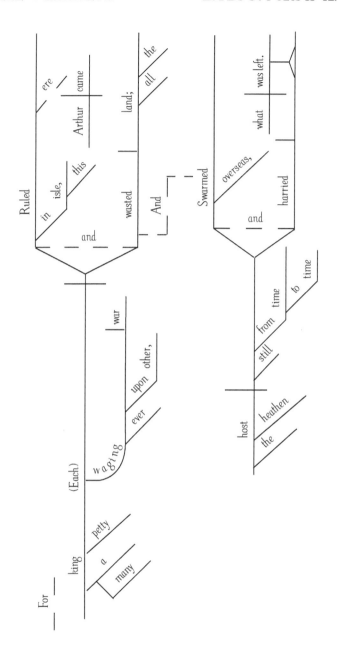

Lesson 24

ℭ

THE PASSING OF KING ARTHUR
from LE MORTE D'ARTHUR by Thomas Malory

But I may not stand, mine head works so. Ah Sir Launcelot, said King Arthur, this day have I sore missed thee: alas, that ever I was against thee, for now have I my death, whereof Sir Gawaine me warned in my dream. Then Sir Lucan took up the king the one part, and Sir Bedivere the other part, and in the lifting the king swooned; and Sir Lucan fell in a swoon with the lift, that the part of his guts fell out of his body, and therewith the noble knight's heart brast. And when the king awoke, he beheld Sir Lucan, how he lay foaming at the mouth, and part of his guts lay at his feet. Alas, said the king, this is to me a full heavy sight, to see this noble duke so die for my sake, for he would have holpen me, that had more need of help than I. Alas, he would not complain him, his heart was so set to help me: now Jesu have mercy upon his soul! Then Sir Bedivere wept for the death of his brother. Leave this mourning and weeping, said the king, for all this will not avail me, for wit thou well an I might live myself, the death of Sir Lucan would grieve me evermore; but my time hieth fast, said the king. Therefore, said Arthur unto Sir Bedivere, take thou Excalibur, my good sword, and go with it to yonder water side, and when thou comest there I charge thee throw my sword in that water, and come again and tell me what thou there seest. My lord, said Bedivere, your commandment shall be done, and lightly bring you word again.

So Sir Bedivere departed, and by the way he beheld that noble sword, that the pommel and the haft was all of precious stones; and then he said to himself: If I throw this rich sword in the water, thereof shall never come good, but harm and loss. And then Sir Bedivere hid Excalibur under a tree. And so, as soon as he might, he came again unto the king, and said he had been at the water, and had thrown the sword in the water. What saw thou there? said the king. Sir, he said, I saw nothing but waves and winds. That is untruly said of thee, said the king, therefore go thou lightly again, and do my commandment; as thou art to me lief and dear, spare not, but throw it in. Then Sir Bedivere returned again, and took the sword in his hand; and then him thought sin and shame to throw away that noble sword, and so eft he hid the sword, and returned again, and told to the king that he had been at the water, and done his commandment. What saw thou there? said the king. Sir, he said, I saw nothing but the waters wap and waves wan. Ah, traitor untrue, said King Arthur, now hast thou betrayed me twice. Who would have weened that, thou that hast been to me so lief and dear? and thou art named a noble knight, and would betray me for the richness of the sword. But now go again lightly, for thy long tarrying putteth me in great jeopardy of my life, for I have taken cold. And but if thou do now as I bid thee, if ever I may see thee, I shall slay thee with mine own hands; for thou wouldst for my rich sword see me dead.

Then Sir Bedivere departed, and went to the sword, and lightly took it up, and went to the water side; and there he bound the girdle about the hilts, and then he threw the sword as far into the water as he might; and there came an arm and an hand above the water and met it, and caught it, and so shook it thrice and brandished, and then vanished away the hand with the sword in the water. So Sir Bedivere came again to the king, and told him what he saw. Alas, said the king, help me hence, for I dread me I have tarried over long. Then Sir Bedivere took the king upon his back, and so went with him to that water side. And when they were at the water side, even fast by the bank hoved a little barge with many fair ladies in it, and among them all was a queen, and all they had black hoods, and all they wept and shrieked when they saw King Arthur. Now put me into the barge, said the king. And so he did softly; and there received him three queens with great mourning; and so they set them down, and in one of their laps King Arthur laid his head. And then that queen said: Ah, dear brother, why have ye tarried so long from me? alas, this wound on your head hath caught over-much cold. And so then they rowed from the land, and Sir Bedivere beheld all those ladies go from him. Then Sir Bedivere cried: Ah my lord Arthur, what shall become of me, now ye go from me and leave me here alone among mine enemies? Comfort thyself, said the king, and do as well as thou mayst,

for in me is no trust for to trust in; for I will into the vale of Avilion
to heal me of my grievous wound: and if thou hear never more of me,
pray for my soul. But ever the queens and ladies wept and shrieked,
that it was pity to hear. And as soon as Sir Bedivere had lost the sight
of the barge, he wept and wailed, and so took the forest; and so he
went all that night, and in the morning he was ware betwixt two holts
hoar, of a chapel and an hermitage.

Lesson 24.1

Prose & Poetry

LITERARY ELEMENTS

3 **Observe the Invention and Arrangement**

◆ **Lyrical Elements**

- Describes

- Senses

- Comparisons

◆ **Narrative Elements**

- **Setting** ancient Britain

- **Characters** King Arthur, Sir Lucan, Sir Bedivere

- **Conflict** King Arthur, knowing he is about to die, asks Sir
  Bedivere to go and throw his sword Excalibur into the water.
  Bedivere hates to lose it forever, and tries to hide it instead.
  Each time he comes back, Arthur knows that he has not
  done what he was asked.

- **Resolution** Bedivere finally throws the sword into the
  lake, and sees an arm and hand catch and brandish it. King
  Arthur is then able to depart for the Isle of Avalon to heal
  his "grievous wound."

- **Sequence** chronological order of events
- **Point of View** 3rd person omniscient

4 Investigate the Context
- ◆ Identify the poem's **Literary Genre**
  - **Genre by literary period** – fifteenth century British retelling of ancient Briton tale
  - **Genre by poetic/narrative category** – see Lesson 23

Lesson 24.2

Language Logic

SENTENCE DIAGRAMMING AND PARSING

[(In after times) [when the King had passed overseas to France, leaving Sir Mordred to rule Britain (in his stead),] there came messengers (from Britain) bearing letters (for King Arthur.)]   – *complex sentence*

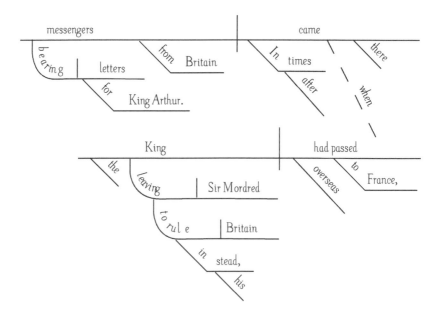

Nota Bene: We have diagrammed *from Britain* as an adjective element describing messengers. It could also be considered an adverb element modifying came. Ask students to consider both options, and choose the way they thinks better reflects the sense of the sentence.

WORD	PART OF SPEECH	DEFINE	CLASSIFY	PROPERTIES	FUNCTION
overseas	adverb	modifies a verb	--	--	modifies *passed*
to rule	verbal	*to rule*	infinitive	--	adverbial; modifies *leaving* (answers why?)
messengers	noun	person	common	3rd plural masculine	subject of principal clause
bearing	verbal	*to bear*	participle	present	modifies *messengers*
letters	noun	thing	common	3rd plural neuter	DO *bearing*

Eloquent Expression

COPIA OF CONSTRUCTION: PARALLELISM

Answers will vary: 1. As he grew to manhood, Arthur was instructed in the arts of war, horsemanship, and courtesy. 2. Arthur won the hearts of his subjects by righting wrongs, fighting injustice, and overcoming oppression. 3. A hand rising from the deep caught the sword, brandished it, and drew it beneath the surface.

Lesson 24.3

Language Logic

SENTENCE DIAGRAMMING AND PARSING

[Then, turning to Sir Bedivere, [who <u>stood</u> sorrowing (beside

him,)] he <u>said,</u> ["<u>Leave</u> weeping now, [for the <u>time</u> <u>is</u> short."]]

– compound-complex sentence

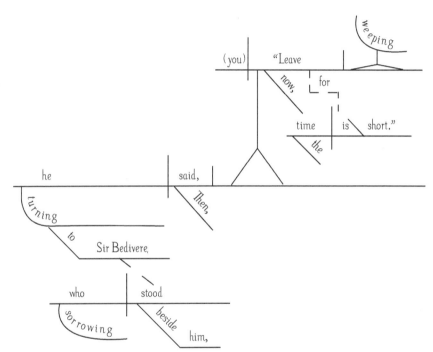

WORD	PART OF SPEECH	DEFINE	CLASSIFY	PROPERTIES	FUNCTION
turning	verbal	*to turn*	participle	present	modifies *he*
who	pronoun	Sir Bedivere	relative	3rd singular masculine	subject of relative clause
sorrowing	verbal	*to sorrow*	participle	present	modifies *who*
beside him	prepositional phrase	relates *him* to *stood*	--	--	adverbial, modifies *stood*
Leave	verb	action	transitive	3rd singular present	main verb of subordinate clause
weeping	verbal	*to weep*	gerund	present	DO *Leave*
there	adverb	modifes a verb	--	--	modifies *sit*

Eloquent Expression

COPIA OF CONSTRUCTION: ANTITHESIS

Answers will vary: Sir Launcelot was a man with remarkable strength of body, yet uncommon humility of spirit. Arthur was an amiable ally, but a fearsome foe. (Bonus points for alliteration!)

Lesson 26

☙

from THE CANTERBURY TALES

When April with his showers sweet with fruit
The drought of March has pierced unto the root
And bathed each vein with liquor that has power
To generate therein and sire the flower;
When Zephyr also has, with his sweet breath,
Quickened again, in every holt and heath,
The tender shoots and buds, and the young sun
Into the Ram one half his course has run,
And many little birds make melody
That sleep through all the night with open eye
(So Nature pricks them on to ramp and rage) –
Then do folk long to go on pilgrimage,
And palmers to go seeking out strange strands,
To distant shrines well known in sundry lands.
And specially from every shire's end
Of England, they to Canterbury wend,
The blessed holy martyr there to seek
Who helped them when they lay so ill and weak.
    Befell that, in that season, on a day
In Southwark, at the Tabard, as I lay
Ready to start upon my pilgrimage
To Canterbury, full of devout homage,
There came at nightfall to that hostelry
Some nine and twenty in a company
Of sundry persons who had chanced to fall
In fellowship, and pilgrims were they all
That toward Canterbury town would ride.
The rooms and stables spacious were and wide,
And well we there were eased, and of the best.

And briefly, when the sun had gone to rest,
So had I spoken with them, every one,
That I was of their fellowship anon,
And made agreement that we'd early rise
To take the road, as you I will apprise.

— GEOFFREY CHAUCER (MODERNIZED BY J.U. NICHOLSON)

൭

Lesson 26.1

Prose & Poetry

LITERARY ELEMENTS

3 Observe the Invention and Arrangement

◆ **Lyrical Elements**

- He describes spring and pilgrimages.

- Sight, sound, touch

- See list of personification and metaphor below.

◆ **Narrative Elements**

- **Point of View** 1st person

4 Investigate the Context

◆ Identify the poem's **Literary Genre**

- **Genre by literary period** – 14th century British
- **Genre by poetic/narrative category** – narrative; the
  Prologue is a narrative set-up for the rest of the poem.

Language Logic

SENTENCE DIAGRAMMING AND PARSING

[[When April (with his showers sweet) (with fruit)

The drought (of March) has pierced (unto the root)

And bathed each vein (with liquor [that has power

To generate therein and sire the flower];

[When Zephyr also has, (with his sweet breath,)

Quickened again, (in every holt and heath,)

The tender shoots and buds,] and [the young sun

(Into the Ram) one half his course has run,]

And [many little birds make melody

[That sleep (through all the night) (with open eye)

[So Nature pricks them (on to ramp and rage)] –

Then do folk long to go (on pilgrimage.)

– compound-complex sentence

Nota Bene: *A plan of attack for this diagram might be to work on the whiteboard or on small pieces of paper, diagramming each clause separately. Then add the conjunctions at the end to put it all together. Alternately, diagram it with the students on the whiteboard in class, but do not allow students to copy the diagram. Rather, have them reproduce it on paper at a later time.*

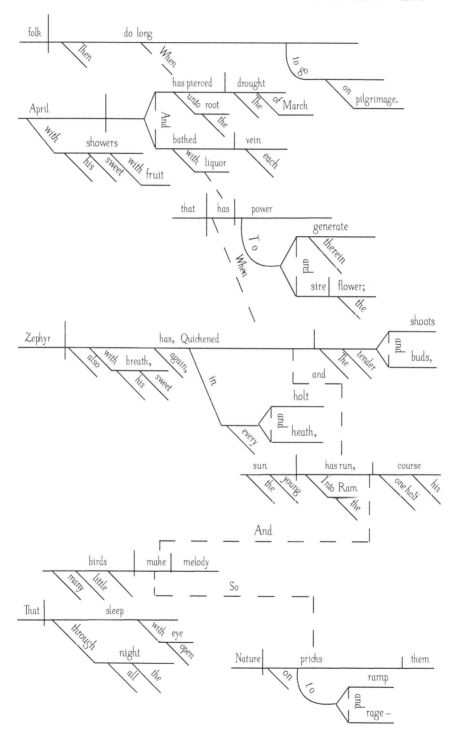

WORD	PART OF SPEECH	DEFINE	CLASSIFY	PROPERTIES	FUNCTION
has pierced	verb	action	transitive	3rd plural present perfect	compound main verb of subordinate clause
unto the root	prepositional phrase	relates *root* to *pierce*	--	--	adverbial, modifies *pierce*
to generate	verbal	*to generate*	verbal	infinitive	adjectival, modifies *power*
also	adverb	modifies a verb	--	--	modifies *breathes*
folk	noun	person	common	3rd plural common	subject of principal clause
pilgrimage	noun	idea	common	3rd plural neuter	OP *to*

Eloquent Expression

FIGURES OF SPEECH IDENTIFICATION
Representative, not exhaustive.

Alliteration: (most obvious) showers sweet, holt – heath, make melody, ramp – rage, pilgrimage – palmers, stranger sands – shrines – sundry – shire's, fall – fellowship, stable spacious

Onomatopoeia: none

Anastrophe: showers sweet, the drought of March has pierced, the young sun into the Ram one half his course was run, they to Canterbury wend, Befell that, the blessed holy martyr there to seek, pilgrims were they all, So had I spoken, we'd early rise

Simile: none

Metaphor: Zephyr = west wind; into the Ram his half course has run = position of the sun

Personification: (most obvious) showers are sweet, showers pierce, drought is pierced, veins are bathed, liquor has power, Zephyr with his sweet breath (west wind), young sun, sun . . . has run, birds making melody, sun had gone to rest

Polysyndeton: All the "and's" connecting the clauses of the first sentence

Asyndeton: none

Parallelism: none

Antithesis: none

Lesson 26.2

Prose & Poetry

SCANSION AND ANALYSIS
Rhyme Scheme: AABBCCDD . . .
Stanza Name: heroic couplet

| ᴗ /| ᴗ / | ᴗ / | ᴗ / | ᴗ / |
When A pril with his show ers sweet with fruit

| ᴗ / | ᴗ / | ᴗ   / | ᴗ /| ᴗ / |
The drought of March has pierced un to the root

| ᴗ / | ᴗ   / | ᴗ / | ᴗ / | ᴗ / |
And bathed each vein with liq uor that has power

|◡ / |◡ / | ◡ / |◡ / |◡ / | |
To gen er ate there in and sire the flower;

| ◡ / |◡ / |◡ / | ◡ / | ◡ / | |
When Zeph yr al so has, with his sweet breath,

| ◡ / |◡ / ◡ / |◡ / |◡ / | |
Quick ened a gain, in ev ery holt and heath,

|◡ / |◡ / |◡ / | ◡ / |◡ / | |
The ten der shoots and buds, and the young sun

|◡/ |◡ / |◡ / |◡ / | ◡ / | |
In to the Ram one half his course has run,

| ◡ / |◡ /|◡ / | ◡ / |◡ / |
And man y lit tle birds make mel o dy

|◡ / | ◡ / |◡ / | ◡ / |◡ / |
That sleep through all the night with o pen eye

| ◡ / | ◡ / | ◡ / |◡ / |◡ / | |
(So Na ture pricks them on to ramp and rage) –

| ◡ / | ◡ / |◡ /|◡ / | ◡ / | |
Then do folk long to go on pil grim age,

| ◡ / |◡ / |◡ / |◡ / | ◡ / | |
And pal mers to go seek ing out strange strands,

|◡ / | ◡ / | ◡ / |◡ / |◡ / | |
To dis tant shrines well known in sun dry lands.

|◡ / |◡ / |◡ / |◡ / |◡ / |
And spe cial ly from ev ery shire's end

|◡ / |◡ / |◡ / |◡ / |◡ / | |
Of Eng land, they to Can ter bur y wend,

| ◡ / |◡ / |◡ / |◡ / |◡ / |
The bles sed ho ly mar tyr there to seek

| ∪   / | ∪   / | ∪   / | ∪ / | ∪   / |

Who helped them when they lay so ill and weak.

Teacher Note: Heroic couplet requires iambic pentameter. Pope's version of *The Odyssey* (Lesson 20) was also written in heroic couplet.

Lesson 25

❧

from THE IDYLLS OF THE KING

And slowly answered Arthur from the barge:
'The old order changeth, yielding place to new,
And God fulfils himself in many ways,
Lest one good custom should corrupt the world.
Comfort thyself: what comfort is in me?
I have lived my life, and that which I have done
May He within himself make pure! but thou,
If thou shouldst never see my face again,
Pray for my soul. More things are wrought by prayer
Than this world dreams of. Wherefore, let thy voice
Rise like a fountain for me night and day.
For what are men better than sheep or goats
That nourish a blind life within the brain,
If, knowing God, they lift not hands of prayer
Both for themselves and those who call them friend?
For so the whole round earth is every way
Bound by gold chains about the feet of God.
But now farewell. I am going a long way
With these thou seest—if indeed I go
(For all my mind is clouded with a doubt)—
To the island-valley of Avilion;
Where falls not hail, or rain, or any snow,
Nor ever wind blows loudly; but it lies
Deep-meadowed, happy, fair with orchard lawns
And bowery hollows crowned with summer sea,
Where I will heal me of my grievous wound.'
So said he, and the barge with oar and sail
Moved from the brink, like some full-breasted swan
That, fluting a wild carol ere her death,
Ruffles her pure cold plume, and takes the flood
With swarthy webs. Long stood Sir Bedivere

Revolving many memories, till the hull
Looked one black dot against the verge of dawn,
And on the mere the wailing died away.

C3

Lesson 25.1

Prose & Poetry

LITERARY ELEMENTS

3 **Observe the Invention and Arrangement**
　◆ **Lyrical Elements**
　　■ Arthur is describing his parting; he describes God's
　　　dominion over the earth, and the island of Avilion
　　■ Primarily sense of sight
　　■ The world is compared to a person that can be corrupted,
　　　and can dream; the voice of his friends is compared to a
　　　fountain, life is compared to a living being that has the
　　　property of vision (blind); Avilion is compared to a person
　　　(happy); the barge is compared to a swan.

　◆ **Narrative Elements**
　　■ **Point of View** this passage is 1st person limited omniscient

4 **Investigate the Context**
　◆ Identify the poem's **Literary Genre**
　　■ **Genre by literary period** – nineteenth century poetic
　　　rendering of an old Briton tale
　　■ **Genre by poetic/narrative category** – narrative

SCANSION:

The meter is predominately iambic pentameter, but there are many variations and irregularities. Ask students to find a couple of lines with regular meter to scan.

The stanza form is blank verse (regular meter, but unrhymed).

Lesson 25.2

Language Logic

SENTENCE DIAGRAMMING AND PARSING

[Here lies Arthur, once King and King to be.]   *– simple sentence*

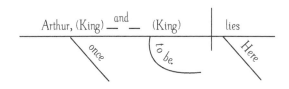

WORD	PART OF SPEECH	DEFINE	CLASSIFY	PROPERTIES	FUNCTION
Here	adverb	modifies a verb	--	--	modifies *lies*
lies	verb	state/ being	intransi- tive	3rd singular present	main verb of sentence
Arthur	noun	person	proper	3rd singular masculine	subject
once	adjective	modifies a noun	--	--	modifies *King*
King	noun	person	proper	3rd singular masculine	appositive, modifiying *Arthur*
and	conjunc- tion	joins two phrases	coordinate	--	joins ap- positive phrases *once King and King to be*

WORD	PART OF SPEECH	DEFINE	CLASSIFY	PROPERTIES	FUNCTION
King	noun	person	proper	3rd singular masculine	appositive, modifying *Arthur*
to be	verbal	*to be*	infinitive	--	adjectival, modifying *King*

Lesson 25.4

ELOQUENT EXPRESSION

LITERARY IMITATION

[Toiling, rejoicing, sorrowing,

  Onward through life he goes,]

[Something attempted, something done,

  Has earned a night's repose.] —— Longfellow, "The Village Blacksmith"

— compound sentence

Figures of description: none; Figures of speech: parallelism and asyndeton, life is referred to metaphorically as a journey (onward through life
he goes . . .)

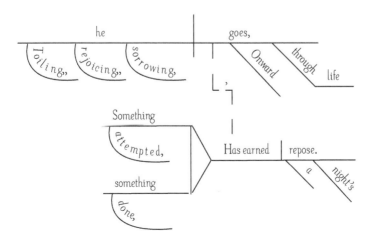

Lesson 27

❧

MACBETH

from TALES FROM SHAKESPEARE **by Charles and Mary Lamb**

[Prologue] When Duncan the Meek reigned King of Scotland, there lived a great thane, or lord, called Macbeth. This Macbeth was a near kinsman to the king, and in great esteem at court for his valour and conduct in the wars; an example of which he had lately given, in defeating a rebel army assisted by the troops of Norway in terrible numbers.

[Action 1] The two Scottish generals, Macbeth and Banquo, returning victorious from this great battle, their way lay over a blasted heath, where they were stopped by the strange appearance of three figures like women, except that they had beards, and their withered skins and wild attire made them look not like any earthly creatures. Macbeth first addressed them, when they, seemingly offended, laid each one her choppy finger upon her skinny lips, in token of silence; and the first of them saluted Macbeth with the title of thane of Glamis. The general was not a little startled to find himself known by such creatures; but how much more, when the second of them followed up that salute by giving him the title of thane of Cawdor, to which honour he had no pretensions; and again the third bid him "All hail! king that shalt be hereafter!" Such a prophetic greeting might well amaze him, who knew that while the king's sons lived he could not hope to succeed to the throne. Then turning to Banquo, they pronounced him, in a sort of riddling terms, to be lesser than Macbeth and greater! not so happy, but much happier! and prophesied that though he should never reign, yet his sons after him should be kings in Scotland. They then turned into air, and vanished: by which the generals knew them to be the weird sisters, or witches.

[Action 2 − Person] While they stood pondering on the strangeness of this adventure, there arrived certain messengers from the king, who were empowered by him to confer upon Macbeth the dignity of thane of Cawdor: an event so miraculously corresponding with the prediction of the witches astonished Macbeth, and he stood wrapped in amazement, unable to make reply to the messengers; and in that point of time swelling hopes arose in his mind that the prediction of the third witch might in like manner have its accomplishment, and that he should one day reign king in Scotland.

Turning to Banquo, he said, "Do you not hope that your children shall be kings, when what the witches promised to me has so wonderfully come to pass?" "That hope," answered the general, "might enkindle you to aim at the throne; but oftentimes these ministers of darkness tell us truths in little things, to betray us into deeds of greatest consequence."

[Explanation] But the wicked suggestions of the witches had sunk too deep into the mind of Macbeth to allow him to attend to the warnings of the good Banquo. From that time he bent all his thoughts how to compass the throne of Scotland.

Macbeth had a wife, to whom he communicated the strange prediction of the weird sisters, and its partial accomplishment. She was a bad, ambitious woman, and so as her husband and herself could arrive at greatness, she cared not much by what means. She spurred on the reluctant purpose of Macbeth, who felt compunction at the thoughts of blood, and did not cease to represent the murder of the king as a step absolutely necessary to the fulfilment of the flattering prophecy.

[Action 3 – Physical, Person] It happened at this time that the king, who out of his royal condescension would oftentimes visit his principal nobility upon gracious terms, came to Macbeth's house, attended by his two sons, Malcolm and Donalbain, and a numerous train of thanes and attendants, the more to honour Macbeth for the triumphal success of his wars.

The castle of Macbeth was pleasantly situated, and the air about it was sweet and wholesome, which appeared by the nests which the martlet, or swallow, had built under all the jutting friezes and buttresses of the building, wherever it found a place of advantage; for where those birds most breed and haunt, the air is observed to be delicate. The king entered well-pleased with the place, and not less so with the attentions and respect of his honoured hostess, Lady

Macbeth, who had the art of covering treacherous purposes with smiles; and could look like the innocent flower, while she was indeed the serpent under it.

[Action 4 – Time, Action, Place] The king being tired with his journey, went early to bed, and in his state-room two grooms of his chamber (as was the custom) slept beside him. He had been unusually pleased with his reception, and had made presents before he retired to his principal officers; and among the rest, had sent a rich diamond to Lady Macbeth, greeting her by the name of his most kind hostess.

[Action 5 – Time, Action] Now was the middle of night, when over half the world nature seems dead, and wicked dreams abuse men's minds asleep, and none but the wolf and the murderer is abroad. This was the time when Lady Macbeth waked to plot the murder of the king. She would not have undertaken a deed so abhorrent to her sex, but that she feared her husband's nature, that it was too full of the milk of human kindness, to do a contrived murder. She knew him to be ambitious, but withal to be scrupulous, and not yet prepared for that height of crime which commonly in the end accompanies inordinate ambition. She had won him to consent to the murder, but she doubted his resolution; and she feared that the natural tenderness of his disposition (more humane than her own) would come between, and defeat the purpose. So with her own hands armed with a dagger, she approached the king's bed; having taken care to ply the grooms of his chamber so with wine, that they slept intoxicated, and careless of their charge. There lay Duncan in a sound sleep after the fatigues of his journey, and as she viewed him earnestly, there was something in his face, as he slept, which resembled her own father; and she had not the courage to proceed.

[Action 6 – Place, Person] She returned to confer with her husband. His resolution had begun to stagger. He considered that there were strong reasons against the deed. In the first place, he was not only a subject, but a near kinsman to the king; and he had been his host and entertainer that day, whose duty, by the laws of hospitality, it was to shut the door against his murderers, not bear the knife himself. Then he considered how just and merciful a king this Duncan had been, how clear of offence to his subjects, how loving to his nobility, and in particular to him; that such kings are the peculiar care of Heaven, and their subjects doubly bound to revenge their deaths. Besides, by the favours of the king, Macbeth stood high in the opinion of all sorts of men, and how would those honours be stained by the reputation of so foul a murder!

[Action 7 – Physical] In these conflicts of the mind Lady Macbeth found her husband inclining to the better part, and resolving to proceed no further. But she being a woman not easily shaken from her evil purpose, began to pour in at his ears words which infused a portion of her own spirit into his mind, assigning reason upon reason why he should not shrink from what he had undertaken; how easy the deed was; how soon it would be over; and how the action of one short night would give to all their nights and days to come sovereign sway and royalty! Then she threw contempt on his change of purpose, and accused him of fickleness and cowardice; and declared that she had given suck, and knew how tender it was to love the babe that milked her; but she would, while it was smiling in her face, have plucked it from her breast, and dashed its brains out, if she had so sworn to do it, as he had sworn to perform that murder. Then she added, how practicable it was to lay the guilt of the deed upon the drunken sleepy grooms. And with the valour of her tongue she so chastised his sluggish resolutions, that he once more summoned up courage to the bloody business.

[Action 8 – Place, Action] So, taking the dagger in his hand, he softly stole in the dark to the room where Duncan lay; and as he went, he thought he saw another dagger in the air, with the handle towards him, and on the blade and at the point of it drops of blood; but when he tried to grasp at it, it was nothing but air, a mere phantasm proceeding from his own hot and oppressed brain and the business he had in hand.

Getting rid of this fear, he entered the king's room, whom he despatched with one stroke of his dagger. Just as he had done the murder, one of the grooms, who slept in the chamber, laughed in his sleep, and the other cried, "Murder," which woke them both; but they said a short prayer; one of them said, "God bless us!" and the other answered "Amen;" and addressed themselves to sleep again. Macbeth, who stood listening to them, tried to say, "Amen," when the fellow said, "God bless us!" but, though he had most need of a blessing, the word stuck in his throat, and he could not pronounce it.

Again he thought he heard a voice which cried, "Sleep no more: Macbeth doth murder sleep, the innocent sleep, that nourishes life." Still it cried, "Sleep no more," to all the house. "Glamis hath murdered sleep, and therefore Cawdor shall sleep no more, Macbeth shall sleep no more."

[Action 9 – Place, Person] With such horrible imaginations Macbeth returned to his listening wife, who began to think he had failed of his purpose, and that the deed was somehow frustrated. He came in so distracted a state, that she reproached him with his want of firmness, and sent him to wash his hands of the blood which stained them, while she took his dagger, with purpose to stain the cheeks of the grooms with blood, to make it seem their guilt.

[Action 10 – Time] Morning came, and with it the discovery of the murder, which could not be concealed; and though Macbeth and his lady made great show of grief, and the proofs against the grooms (the dagger being produced against them and their faces smeared with blood) were sufficiently strong, yet the entire suspicion fell upon Macbeth, whose inducements to such a deed were so much more forcible than such poor silly grooms could be supposed to have; and Duncan's two sons fled. Malcolm, the eldest, sought for refuge in the English court; and the youngest, Donalbain, made his escape to Ireland.

[Explanation] The king's sons, who should have succeeded him, having thus vacated the throne, Macbeth as next heir was crowned king, and thus the prediction of the weird sisters was literally accomplished.

[Description] Though placed so high, Macbeth and his queen could not forget the prophecy of the weird sisters, that, though Macbeth should be king, yet not his children, but the children of Banquo, should be kings after him. The thought of this, and that they had defiled their hands with blood, and done so great crimes, only to place the posterity of Banquo upon the throne, so rankled within them, that they determined to put to death both Banquo and his son, to make void the predictions of the weird sisters, which in their own case had been so remarkably brought to pass.

[Action 11 – Time, Action, Person] For this purpose they made a great supper, to which they invited all the chief thanes; and, among the rest, with marks of particular respect, Banquo and his son Fleance were invited. The way by which Banquo was to pass to the palace at night was beset by murderers appointed by Macbeth, who stabbed Banquo; but in the scuffle Fleance escaped. [author's commentary] From that Fleance descended a race of monarchs who afterwards filled the Scottish throne, ending with James the Sixth of Scotland and the First of England, under whom the two crowns of England and Scotland were united.

[Action 12 – Person, Action, Place] At supper, the queen, whose manners were in the highest degree affable and royal, played the hostess with a gracefulness and attention which conciliated every one present, and Macbeth discoursed freely with his thanes and nobles, saying, that all that was honourable in the country was under his roof, if he had but his good friend Banquo present, whom yet he hoped he should rather have to chide for neglect, than to lament for any mischance. Just at these words the ghost of Banquo, whom he had caused to be murdered, entered the room and placed himself on the chair which Macbeth was about to occupy. Though Macbeth was a bold man, and one that could have faced the devil without trembling, at this horrible sight his cheeks turned white with fear, and he stood quite unmanned with his eyes fixed upon the ghost. His queen and all the nobles, who saw nothing, but perceived him gazing (as they thought) upon an empty chair, took it for a fit of distraction; and she reproached him, whispering that it was but the same fancy which made him see the dagger in the air, when he was about to kill Duncan. But Macbeth continued to see the ghost, and gave no heed to all they could say, while he addressed it with distracted words, yet so significant, that his queen, fearing the dreadful secret would be disclosed, in great haste dismissed the guests, excusing the infirmity of Macbeth as a disorder he was often troubled with.

[Description/Summary] To such dreadful fancies Macbeth was subject. His queen and he had their sleeps afflicted with terrible dreams, and the blood of Banquo troubled them not more than the escape of Fleance, whom now they looked upon as father to a line of kings who should keep their posterity out of the throne. With these miserable thoughts they found no peace, and Macbeth determined once more to seek out the weird sisters, and know from them the worst.

[Action 13 — Person, Place] He sought them in a cave upon the heath, where they, who knew by foresight of his coming, were engaged in preparing their dreadful charms, by which they conjured up infernal spirits to reveal to them futurity. Their horrid ingredients were toads, bats, and serpents, the eye of a newt, and the tongue of a dog, the leg of a lizard, and the wing of the night-owl, the scale of a dragon, the tooth of a wolf, the maw of the ravenous salt-sea shark, the mummy of a witch, the root of the poisonous hemlock (this to have effect must be digged in the dark), the gall of a goat, and the liver of a Jew, with slips of the yew tree that roots itself in graves, and the finger of a dead child: all these were set on to boil in a great kettle, or cauldron, which, as fast as it grew too hot, was cooled with a baboon's blood: to these they poured in the blood of a sow that had eaten her young, and they threw into the flame the grease that had sweaten from a murderer's gibbet. By these charms they bound the infernal spirits to answer their questions.

It was demanded of Macbeth, whether he would have his doubts resolved by them, or by their masters, the spirits. He, nothing daunted by the dreadful ceremonies which he saw, boldly answered, "Where are they? let me see them." [Action 14 — Person] And they called the spirits, which were three. And the first arose in the like-ness of an armed head, and he called Macbeth by name, and bid him beware of the thane of Fife; for which caution Macbeth thanked him; for Macbeth had entertained a jealousy of Macduff, the thane of Fife.

[Action 15 — Person] And the second spirit arose in the like-ness of a bloody child, and he called Macbeth by name, and bid him have no fear, but laugh to scorn the power of man, for none of woman born should have power to hurt him; and he advised him to be bloody, bold, and resolute. "Then live, Macduff!" cried the king; "what need I fear of thee? but yet I will make assurance doubly sure. Thou shalt not live; that I may tell pale-hearted Fear it lies, and sleep in spite of thunder."

[Action 16 — Person] That spirit being dismissed, a third arose in the form of a child crowned, with a tree in his hand. He called Macbeth by name, and comforted him against conspiracies, say-ing, that he should never be vanquished, until the wood of Birnam to Dunsinane Hill should come against him. "Sweet bodements! good!" cried Macbeth; "who can unfix the forest, and move it from its earth-bound roots? I see I shall live the usual period of man's life, and not be cut off by a violent death. But my heart throbs to know one thing. Tell me, if your art can tell so much, if Banquo's issue shall ever reign in this kingdom?" Here the cauldron sank into the ground, and a noise of music was heard, and eight shadows, like kings, passed by Macbeth, and Banquo last, who bore a glass which showed the figures of many more, and Banquo all bloody smiled upon Macbeth, and pointed to them; by which Macbeth knew that these were the posterity of Banquo, who should reign after him in Scotland; and the witches, with a sound of soft music, and with dancing, making a show of duty and welcome to Macbeth, vanished. [Action 17 – manner, person, place] And from this time the thoughts of Macbeth were all bloody and dreadful.

The first thing he heard when he got out of the witches' cave, was that Macduff, thane of Fife, had fled to England, to join the army which was forming against him under Malcolm, the eldest son of the late king, with intent to displace Macbeth, and set Malcolm, the right heir, upon the throne. Macbeth, stung with rage, set upon the castle of Macduff, and put his wife and children, whom the thane had left behind, to the sword, and extended the slaughter to all who claimed the least relationship to Macduff.

[Transition, Description] These and such-like deeds alienated the minds of all his chief nobility from him. Such as could, fled to join with Malcolm and Macduff, who were now approaching with a powerful army, which they had raised in England; and the rest secretly wished success to their arms, though for fear of Macbeth they could take no active part. His recruits went on slowly. Everybody hated the tyrant; nobody loved or honoured him; but all suspected him, and he began to envy the condition of Duncan, whom he had murdered, who slept soundly in his grave, against whom treason had done its worst: steel nor poison, domestic malice nor foreign levies, could hurt him any longer.

[Action 18 – Person, Action] While these things were acting, the queen, who had been the sole partner in his wickedness, in whose bosom he could sometimes seek a momentary repose from those terrible dreams which afflicted them both nightly, died, it is supposed, by her own hands, unable to bear the remorse of guilt, and public hate; by which event he was left alone, without a soul to love or care for him, or a friend to whom he could confide his wicked purposes.

[Action 19 – Manner] He grew careless of life, and wished for death; but the near approach of Malcolm's army roused in him what remained of his ancient courage, and he determined to die (as he expressed it) "with armour on his back." Besides this, the hollow promises of the witches had filled him with a false confidence, and he remembered the sayings of the spirits, that none of woman born was to hurt him, and that he was never to be vanquished till Birnam wood should come to Dunsinane, which he thought could never be. So he shut himself up in his castle, whose impregnable strength was such as defied a siege: here he sullenly waited the approach of Malcolm. [Action 20 – Physical] When, upon a day, there came a messenger to him, pale and shaking with fear, almost unable to report that which he had seen; for he averred, that as he stood upon his watch on the hill, he looked towards Birnam, and to his thinking the wood began to move! "Liar and slave!" cried Macbeth; "if thou speakest false, thou shalt hang alive upon the next tree, till famine end thee. If thy tale be true, I care not if thou dost as much by me;" for Macbeth now began to faint in resolution, and to doubt the equivocal speeches of the spirits. He was not to fear till Birnam wood should come to Dunsinane; and now a wood did move! "However," said he, "if this which he avouches be true, let us arm and out. There is no flying hence, nor staying here. I begin to be weary of the sun, and wish my life at an end." With these desperate speeches he sallied forth upon the besiegers, who had now come up to the castle.

[Action 21 – Person, Place] The strange appearance which had given the messenger an idea of a wood moving is easily solved. When the besieging army marched through the wood of Birnam, Malcolm, like a skilful general, instructed his soldiers to hew down every one a bough and bear it before him, by way of concealing the true numbers of his host. This marching of the soldiers with boughs had at a distance the appearance which had frightened the mes-senger. Thus were the words of the spirit brought to pass, in a sense different from that in which Macbeth had understood them, and one great hold of his confidence was gone.

[Action 22 – Person, Action] And now a severe skirmishing took place, in which Macbeth, though feebly supported by those who called themselves his friends, but in reality hated the tyrant and inclined to the party of Malcolm and Macduff, yet fought with the extreme of rage and valour, cutting to pieces all who were opposed to him, till he came to where Macduff was fighting. Seeing Macduff, and remembering the caution of the spirit who had counselled him to avoid Macduff, above all men, he would have turned, but Macduff, who had been seeking him through the whole fight, opposed his turning, and a fierce contest ensued; Macduff giving him many foul reproaches for the murder of his wife and children. Macbeth, whose soul was charged enough with blood of that family already, would still have declined the combat; but Macduff still urged him to it, calling him tyrant, murderer, hell-hound, and villain.

[Action 23 – Manner] Then Macbeth remembered the words of the spirit, how none of woman born should hurt him; and smiling confidently he said to Macduff, "Thou losest thy labour, Macduff. As easily thou mayest impress the air with thy sword, as make me vulnerable. I bear a charmed life, which must not yield to one of woman born."

"Despair thy charm," said Macduff, "and let that lying spirit whom thou hast served, tell thee, that Macduff was never born of woman, never as the ordinary manner of men is to be born, but was untimely taken from his mother."

[Action 24 – Manner] Accursed be the tongue which tells me so," said the trembling Macbeth, who felt his last hold of confidence give way; "and let never man in future believe the lying equivocations of witches and juggling spirits, who deceive us in words which have double senses, and while they keep their promise literally, disappoint our hopes with a different meaning. I will not fight with thee."

"Then live!" said the scornful Macduff; "we will have a show of thee, as men show monsters, and a painted board, on which shall be written, 'Here men may see the tyrant!'"

[Action 25 – Manner, Action] "Never," said Macbeth, whose courage returned with despair; "I will not live to kiss the ground before young Malcolm's feet, and to be baited with the curses of the rabble. Though Birnam wood be come to Dunsinane, and thou opposed to me, who wast never born of woman, yet will I try the last." With these frantic words he threw himself upon Macduff, who, after a severe struggle, in the end overcame him, and cutting off his head, [Action 26 – Person, Action] made a present of it to the young and lawful king, Malcolm; who took upon him the government which, by the machinations of the usurper, he had so long been deprived of, and ascended the throne of Duncan the Meek, amid the acclamations of the nobles and the people.

☙

Lesson 27.1

Prose & Poetry

LITERARY ELEMENTS

3 **Observe the Invention and Arrangement**
 ◆ **Lyrical Elements**

- Describes
- Senses
- Comparisons

◆ **Narrative Elements**

- **Setting** Scotland, 11th century
- **Characters** witches, Macbeth, Lady Macbeth, Banquo, Macduff, Malcolm, Duncan, Banquo's ghost, Fleance
- **Conflict** Macbeth is ambitious to be king.
- **Resolution** Macbeth kills Macduff at Lady Macbeth's goading, and becomes king. Eventually guilt drives him to additional murders, and her to madness and suicide. Macbeth is eventually killed by his own men and the rightful heir, Malcolm, takes back the throne.
- **Sequence** *in medias res*, with Macbeth as a full-grown man, but the plot is linear from that point forward.

■ **Point of View** Third person omniscient

4 Investigate the Context

◆ Identify the poem's **Literary Genre**

■ **Genre by literary period** – 19th century retelling of an early 17th century play adapted from the life of an historical Scottish king

■ **Genre by poetic/narrative category** – fiction, based on an historical narrative

---

Lesson 27.2

Prose & Poetry

NARRATIVE PLOT ANALYSIS

See suggested scene divisions in selection at beginning of this lesson. Remember that answers may vary.

Lesson 27.3

Language Logic

SENTENCE DIAGRAMMING AND PARSING

[She spurred on the reluctant purpose (of Macbeth,) [who felt compunction (at the thoughts) (of blood,)] and did not cease to represent the murder (of the king) (as a step absolutely necessary) (to the fulfilment) (of the flattering prophecy.)]   – *compound-complex sentence*

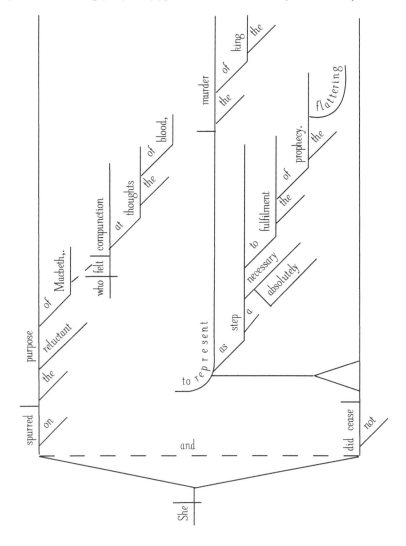

WORD	PART OF SPEECH	DEFINE	CLASSIFY	PROPERTIES	FUNCTION
purpose	noun	idea	common	3rd singular neuter	DO *spurred*
Macbeth	noun	person	proper	3rd singular masculine	OP *of*
did cease	verb	action	transitive	3rd singular	compound main verb of principal clause
flattering	verbal	*to flatter*	participle	present	modifies *prophecy*

Lesson 27.5

Eloquent Expression

LITERARY IMITATION

[Life's but a walking shadow, a poor player [that struts and frets his hour
(upon the stage) and then is heard no more]]: [it is a tale told (by an
idiot,) full (of sound and fury), signifying nothing.] —Macbeth, Act V,
Scene 5   *— compound-complex sentence*

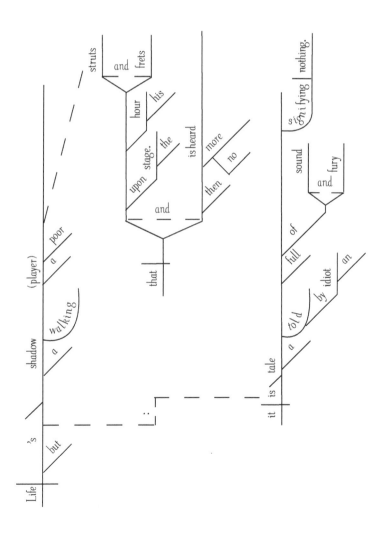

Lesson 28

❧

A Heath Near Forres

from MACBETH by William Shakespeare

MACBETH

> So foul and fair a day I have not seen.

BANQUO

> How far is't call'd to Forres? What are these
> So wither'd and so wild in their attire,
> That look not like the inhabitants o' the earth,
> And yet are on't? Live you? or are you aught
> That man may question? You seem to understand me,
> By each at once her chappy finger laying
> Upon her skinny lips: you should be women,
> And yet your beards forbid me to interpret
> That you are so.

MACBETH

> Speak, if you can: what are you?

First Witch

> All hail, Macbeth! hail to thee, thane of Glamis!

Second Witch

> All hail, Macbeth, hail to thee, thane of Cawdor!

Third Witch

> All hail, Macbeth, thou shalt be king hereafter!

BANQUO

> Good sir, why do you start; and seem to fear
> Things that do sound so fair? I' the name of truth,
> Are ye fantastical, or that indeed

Which outwardly ye show? My noble partner
You greet with present grace and great prediction
Of noble having and of royal hope,
That he seems rapt withal: to me you speak not.
If you can look into the seeds of time,
And say which grain will grow and which will not,
Speak then to me, who neither beg nor fear
Your favours nor your hate.

First Witch

Hail!

Second Witch

Hail!

Third Witch

Hail!

First Witch

Lesser than Macbeth, and greater.

Second Witch

Not so happy, yet much happier.

Third Witch

Thou shalt get kings, though thou be none:
So all hail, Macbeth and Banquo!

First Witch

Banquo and Macbeth, all hail!

MACBETH

Stay, you imperfect speakers, tell me more:
By Sinel's death I know I am thane of Glamis;
But how of Cawdor? the thane of Cawdor lives,
A prosperous gentleman; and to be king
Stands not within the prospect of belief,
No more than to be Cawdor. Say from whence
You owe this strange intelligence? or why
Upon this blasted heath you stop our way

With such prophetic greeting? Speak, I charge you.

Witches vanish

BANQUO

The earth hath bubbles, as the water has,
And these are of them. Whither are they vanish'd?

MACBETH

Into the air; and what seem'd corporal melted
As breath into the wind. Would they had stay'd!

BANQUO

Were such things here as we do speak about?
Or have we eaten on the insane root
That takes the reason prisoner?

MACBETH

Your children shall be kings.

BANQUO

You shall be king.

MACBETH

And thane of Cawdor too: went it not so?

BANQUO

To the selfsame tune and words.

— ACT 1, SCENE 3, LINES 36-86

ℭℜ

Lesson 28.1

Prose & Poetry

LITERARY ELEMENTS SEE LESSON 27

3 **Observe the Invention and Arrangement**
◆ **Narrative Elements**

- ■ **Setting** a wood near Forres
- ■ **Characters** Macbeth, Banquo, witches

SCANSION

Some lines, such as the witches' greeting to Macbeth, are in iambic pentameter.

Lesson 28.2

Language Logic

SENTENCE DIAGRAMMING AND PARSING

[Everybody hated the tyrant;] [nobody loved or honoured him;] but [all suspected him,] and [he envied the condition of Duncan, [whom he had murdered,] [who slept soundly in his grave,] [against whom treason had done its worst]]: [steel nor poison, domestic malice nor foreign levies, could hurt him any longer.]   *– compound-complex sentence*

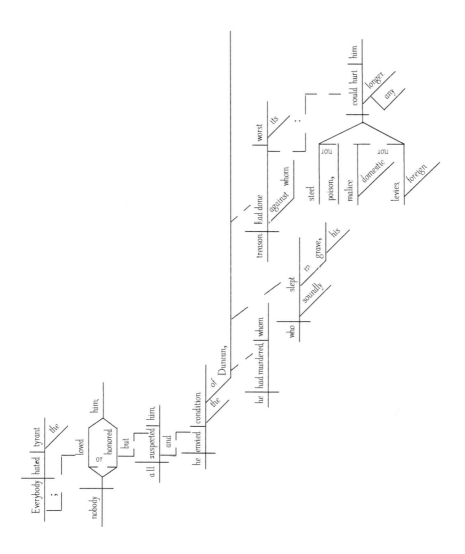

WORD	PART OF SPEECH	DEFINE	CLASSIFY	PROPERTIES	FUNCTION
Everybody	pronoun	stands in for Macbeth's subjects	personal	3rd plural common	subject of principal clause
whom (he had murdered)	pronoun	stands in for *Duncan*	relative	3rd plural masculine	DO *had murdered*
who	pronoun	stands in for *Duncan*	relative	3rd plural masculine	subject of principal clause
(against) whom	pronoun	stands in for *Duncan*	relative	3rd plural masculine	OP *against*
worst	adjective	modifies a (missing) noun	descriptive	--	used substantively as DO *had done*
malice	noun	thing	common	3rd singular neuter	compound subject of principal clause
could hurt	verb	action	transitive	3rd singular present	compound main verb of principal clause

Appendix

GRAMMAR REVIEW

For use as needed, before beginning *Bards & Poets II*.

If your student has not previously studied English Grammar, spend at least a week, or even up to a month, on basic grammar concepts. Here is a suggested plan:

A. Follow the instructions in the Appendix of the Student Book to set up a flashcard review system. Consider having your student make flashcards by hand. Introduce and study all of the shaded terms in Grammar Terms and Defintions (Appendix of the Student Book).

B. Study these lessons in *Sentence Sense* to introduce the Parts of Speech:
    - 1.0A, 1.0B, and 1.1 The Noun
    - 2.0A and 2.1 The Pronoun
    - 3.0A and 3.1 The Verb
    - 4.0A and 4.1 The Adjective
    - 5.0 and 5.1A The Adverb
    - 6.0 and 6.1A The Preposition
    - 7.0 and 7.1A The Conjunction
    - 8.1 The Interjection

C. Study the rest of the review lessons in *Sentence Sense* listed in each of the Language Logic sections of Lessons 1 & 2 in the Student Book covering the parts of speech, basic sentence construction, and basic sentence diagramming.

D. Complete the Harvey's Exercise 19 below to practice identifying parts of speech in sentences. You may also use Harvey's Exercises 153.1-153.4 in *Sentence Sense* for some additional practice if needed.

HARVEY'S EXERCISE 19

Only review as much as your student needs. You may wish to do just a few from each section over several days. This makes a good classroom exercise as well.

Exercise #5

1. I (PRO) do not know where you (PRO) live.

2. Who (PRO) gave her (PRO) that pencil (N)?

3. She (PRO) came from home (N) an hour (N) ago.

4. What (PRO) have you (PRO) there, my (PRO) son (N)?

5. Their (PRO) house (N) is much larger than our (PRO) uncle's. (N)

6. Your (PRO) father (N) is her (PRO) mother's (N) brother.

7. Whose (PRO) farm (N) is for sale in your (PRO) neighborhood? (N)

Exercise #6

1. The farmer (N) plows (V) in the spring (N) and fall (N).

2. Their (PRO) father (N) gave (V) them (PRO) money (N).

3. The great tears (N) sprang (V) to their (PRO) eyes (N).

4. They (PRO) followed (V) the cattle (N) home (N).

5. The landlord (N) answered (V) his (PRO) question (N).

6. He (PRO) ordered (V) him (PRO) to go.

7. The pupils (N) who (PRO) had (V) passed (V) a good examination (N), went (V) home (N) with joyful hearts. (N)

Exercise #8

1. He who gives (V) cheerfully gives twice. (ADV)

2. His affairs were (V) managed (V) imprudently (ADV).

3. Proceed (V) slowly (ADV) and cautiously. (ADV)

4. We shall (V) never (ADV) see (V) his like again. (ADV)

5. You have (V) not (ADV) acted (V) wisely. (ADV)

6. We must (V) study (V) diligently. (ADV)

7. Our dinner, cooked* hastily, (ADV) was (V) eaten (V) greedily. (ADV)

Cooked is a verbal (participle) here. If a student identifies this as a verb or an adjective, simply explain that it *cooked* is a verb used as an adjective here, and we will learn more about this later.

Exercise #9

1. The boy fell over (PREP) a chair into (PREP) a tub of water.

2. I came from (PREP) Boston to (PREP) Cincinnati in (PREP) 1875.

3. We rested by (PREP) the road-side.

4. He walked up (PREP) the valley towards (PREP) the house of (PREP) his friend.

5. Walk with (PREP) me in (PREP) the garden.

6. I went to (PREP) the doctor fo (PREP) r advice, but he was not at (PREP) home.

Exercise #10

1. He is wise and (CONJ) prudent.

2. James or (CONJ) John will call upon (PREP) you.

3. I study because (CONJ) I wish to learn.

4. Neither Jane nor (CONJ) Sarah was in (PREP) the room.

5. I shall not go, if (CONJ) it rain.

6.   He is rich, but (CONJ) is very unhappy.

7.   Worship the Lord, for (CONJ) he is our God.

Exercise #11

1. Hurrah! (INT) we have won!

2. Pshaw, (INT) that is nonsense.

3. Ha, ha, ha! (INT) I am glad of it.

4. Ahem! (INT) did he say so?

5. "0," (INT) said John.

6. What! (INT) tired so soon ?Bibliography

Bibliography

Cℛ

This Bibliography lists works that we have used in researching and creating this curriculum. Most of these are cited by short footnotes throughout the text. Most selections at the beginning of lessons are in the public domain, besides the full length excerpts of the progymnasmata translations, which are used by permission of the Society for Biblical Literature in Atlanta, Georgia.

Erasmus, *On Copia of Words and Ideas*, trans. Donald B. King. Milwaukee: The Marquette University Press, 1963.

Gayley, Young, and Kurtz, *English Poetry: Its Principles and Progress.* New York: The Macmillan Company, 1921.

Gideon O. Burt. Silva Rhetoricae, http://rhetoric.byu.edu/

Gibson, Craig A. *Libanius' Progymnasmata: Model Exercises in Greek Prose Composition and Rhetoric.* Atlanta, Society for Biblical Literature, 2008.

Harvey, Thomas W. *A Practical Grammar of the English Language: Revised Edition.* New York: Van Antwerp, Bragg & Co., 1868.

Harvey, Thomas W. *Elementary Grammar and Composition.* New York: American Book Compar, 1880.

Kennedy, George A. *Progymnasmata: Greek Textbooks of Prose Composition and Rhetoric.* Atlanta: Society of Biblical Literature, 2003.

Hock, Ronald F., and O'Neil, Edward N. *The Chreia and Ancient*

Rhetoric: Classroom Exercises. Atlanta, Society for Biblical Literature, 2002.

Cʒ